MW00440582

PARALLEL JUSTICE FOR VICTIMS OF CRIME

SUSAN HERMAN

THE NATIONAL CENTER FOR VICTIMS OF CRIME | WASHINGTON, DC

PARALLEL JUSTICE FOR VICTIMS OF CRIME
Copyright © 2010 Susan Herman

For permissions, information, or to order additional copies, please contact the Parallel Justice Project at **www.paralleljustice.org**.

Book design by Michael Brechner / Cypress House
Cover design by JamArtz

PUBLISHER'S CATALOGING-IN-PUBLICATION DATA

Herman, Susan.
    Parallel justice for victims of crime / Susan Herman. -- 1st ed. --
Washington, DC : National Center for Victims of Crime, c2010.
    p. ; cm.
    ISBN: 978-0-615-32610-8
    Includes index.
    1. Victims of crimes--United States. 2. Victims of crimes--
Services for--United States. 3. Criminal justice, Administration of--
United States. 4. Restorative justice--United States. 5. Law reform-
-United States. I. National Center for Victims of Crime (U.S.)
II. Title.

    HV6250.3.U5 H46 2010   2009938598
    362.88/0973--dc22 1001

PRINTED IN THE UNITED STATES
9 8 7 6 5 4 3 2
FIRST EDITION

FSC
www.fsc.org
MIX
Paper from
responsible sources
FSC® C011935

To my mother,
Marion Seamon Herman,
for a thousand reasons,
and to my father,
John R. Herman,
for just as many.

Contents

Preface

Toward a New Vision of Justice for Victims of Crime

IN 1977, I SPENT A YEAR TEACHING SELF-DEFENSE to rape crisis counselors at Women Organized Against Rape in Philadelphia, one of the first rape crisis organizations in the country. Three times a week we turned a small meeting room into a dojo, and practiced techniques that often reminded the students of the assaults they had survived. On the mats, holding, throwing, and encouraging these women, most of whom had been raped or abused, I learned that some could not bear to have hands near their necks, some cried whenever they were on their backs, some couldn't control anger that erupted without warning.

I saw how traumatic and destructive the impact of violence can be. Despite the fact that these women wanted to end the secrecy and shame attached to sexual assault, most of them had told no one, not even each other, that they had been victims. One by one they identified fears and vulnerabilities and pushed through them. While these women understood that rape was not their fault, they did not want to be told they were safe, that it would never happen again. They wouldn't have believed me. They knew this was a guarantee no one could make. Instead, they wanted to do as much as they could to heal their wounds, take control of their lives, and learn how to reduce the likelihood they would be raped again.

I wanted to help them get their lives back on track. I also knew that each of them deserved justice, something they all hoped to gain for the women and girls they spoke with on hotlines and saw in emergency rooms and courts every day, but something few of them could imagine for themselves.

This book was inspired by these women and countless other people who have been victims of crime. I have been a victim advocate, in one form or another, for over thirty years. In addition to teaching self-defense to rape crisis counselors, I have established shelters, emergency daycare, and detox programs for battered women, and have overseen the development of the New York City Police Department's policies on domestic violence and child abuse. I have mediated disputes involving victims who experienced a range of misdemeanors and felonies, and have counseled survivors of the September 11 attacks.

In every case, I came to a profoundly disturbing conclusion: While the trauma and harm experienced by many victims of crime is deep, debilitating, and long-lasting, our treatment of crime victims at every level—individual, community, and governmental—is ineffective, fragmented, and dismissive. This woefully inadequate response reinforces victims' sense of shame and isolation, and a misguided belief that recovery is a private matter.

Given the extent of the harm caused by crime, and the millions of walking wounded who live far less than happy and healthy lives, our collective failure to respond to their needs is a national disgrace. We understood better how to respond to the victims of the September 11 attacks. We rallied for them as soon as possible, offering emotional support and an unprecedented range of resources and assistance. But every year crime wreaks havoc on millions of Americans' lives, and we have yet to respond with comparable compassion and creativity.

Surely justice requires more than holding offenders accountable. Yet we minimize victims' pain and suffering, and pretend that criminal convictions are a sufficient balm. We ask crime victims to adjust, to move on with their lives, or worse, to live in secrecy, and to individually manage what may be their greatest emotional, psychological, and financial needs, at a time when some assistance could make all the difference. We know the consequences of crime and violence. We know that crime destroys the sense of trust and safety that keeps people and communities healthy and thriving. But we don't connect the dots, and our failure to respond to victims of crime is a daily injustice.

During the seven and a half years I served as the executive director of the National Center for Victims of Crime, I began to imagine a separate pathway to justice for victims. I called this new framework Parallel Justice to emphasize that our obligations to victims exist apart from our separate commitments to hold offenders accountable. I imagined a world in which we articulated a set of principles that guided our interactions with victims. I imagined new ways for our criminal justice agencies, our healthcare and social service providers, our businesses, and our neighbors, to all contribute to justice for victims of crime.

Since 2000, when I received a wonderful invitation to showcase Parallel Justice at the National Press Club, I have had the opportunity to introduce this new concept at conferences all over the world. I'm pleased to say that the idea has begun to take hold in several communities. People in a wide variety of positions, including police chiefs, corrections officials, and victim advocates, have led Parallel Justice initiatives. From Vermont to California, and Germany to New Zealand, the idea that victims deserve justice, a communal commitment to keep them safe and help them rebuild their lives — regardless of whether an offender is ever identified or prosecuted—has been well received.

This book is for victims of crime, as well as victim advocates, criminal justice and social service practitioners, policymakers, academics, government and community-based leaders, and anyone else who wants to understand how we might achieve justice for victims of crime. I hope that the chapters that follow lead readers to two conclusions: First, that we have failed to provide justice to crime victims, and that this failure has profound and lasting consequences for them, their families, and their communities; and second, that Parallel Justice offers a vision that can lead our country to a new reality in which victims of crime are afforded justice.

⊣ | | | ⊢

Introduction

The Parallel Justice Idea

AFTER A CRIME HAS BEEN COMMITTED, how do we know when justice has been served? In most cases, a crime produces both an offender and a victim. Traditionally, however, when we ask whether justice has been achieved, we focus solely on the offender. We embrace the obligation to bring an offender to the bar of justice, determine whether he has violated the law, and if so, sanction him with fines, probation, imprisonment, or even death. Our criminal justice process can be viewed as a communal response to the offender that says, "If you violate the law, we will hold you accountable, punish you if appropriate, isolate you if needed, and offer you services to help reintegrate you into the community." If this process is fair to the offender, sanctions are proportional to the crime, and the outcome is in the best interest of society at large, we say that justice has been served.

But has it?

For the victims of crime, there is no comparable communal response. There is no acknowledgment that says, "What happened to you was wrong." There is no obligation to say, "We will help you rebuild your life." In short, there is no societal commitment to achieve justice for victims.

The concept of Parallel Justice is rooted in the belief that society has an obligation to provide justice to victims. When a crime has occurred, the social contract has been breached, and true justice requires attention to the needs of those who have suffered, as well as those who violated the law. A just society would seek to heal the wounds that crime has caused, keep victims safe, and empower them to reengage fully in society.

Securing criminal convictions and holding offenders accountable can never fully achieve these goals. Consider these examples: A woman who has been mugged, and now is too afraid to leave her home to buy food or go to work, needs counseling and assistance with transportation. The bank teller who was robbed at gunpoint, and now can no longer face going to work, needs job training to start a new career. The elderly victim of identity theft who lost his entire life savings and cannot possibly earn it back needs financial assistance. The battered woman who wants desperately to leave her violent home needs a job, daycare, and new housing. The young victim of sexual assault, incest, or child abuse who has begun to use drugs to numb the pain needs drug treatment. A burglary victim who feels the police minimized the crime because his losses are covered by insurance, and is angry because the police never caught the offender, simply wants the opportunity to describe his experience to a government official who will acknowledge that what happened to him was wrong.

Parallel Justice represents a fundamental shift in the way our society responds to crime. For victims of crime, and for those who interact with them, including victim advocates, police officers, healthcare providers, religious leaders, social workers, neighbors, attorneys, judges, and elected officials, Parallel Justice offers a more expansive way to think about justice, challenging society to respond to victims of crime with a greater degree of commitment and humanity.

Parallel Justice requires a focused, communal effort that is fair, equitable, and tailored to meet the needs of individual victims. While such a response aids victims of crime, it would also have enormous benefits for society at large, including overall reductions in crime, physical and mental illness, substance abuse, social isolation, and community breakdown.

The concept of Parallel Justice also affirms society's obligation to keep its citizens safe, and our special obligation to protect those citizens who have been harmed from incurring further harm. When a crime occurs, and someone is in danger as a result, his or her need for safety creates a heightened obligation on the part of government to intervene. Research has established that crime leaves victims vulnerable to more crime.[1] This phenomenon, known as repeat victimization, has been documented across several categories of crime. Once people in intimate relationships have been battered, they are more likely to be battered again. Once a home has been burglarized, it is more likely to be targeted again.

Following the principles of Parallel Justice, we should respond to the phenomenon of repeat victimization by developing a range of relocation options for victims of domestic violence and stalking, enhancing the security of burglary victims, and working with all victims of crime to reduce their vulnerability to further crime. We should help these victims, in part, to honor our obligation to protect our fellow citizens, and particularly the most vulnerable among us. If we meet this obligation, we will reduce crime and promote public safety.

This obligation to protect our citizens has another dimension. Research has revealed a link between victimization and future criminal behavior. Children who have been victims of abuse and neglect are more likely to commit delinquent and criminal acts.[2] Among teenagers, the strongest predictor of future criminal behavior is a prior experience as a crime victim.[3] These studies demonstrate that helping victims may also turn out to be one of the most effective ways to prevent further crime and violence.

In describing the contours of a parallel path to justice for victims, this book builds on over three decades of experience by victim advocates across the country. Regardless of whether they work with all crime victims, or with victims of a particular crime such as incest, identity theft, sexual assault, drunk driving, burglary, homicide, domestic violence, fraud, or hate crime, all advocates recognize three salient needs of crime victims: first, victims need to be safe; second, they need to recover from the trauma of the crime; and third, they need to regain control of their lives. The pursuit of justice requires us to address these three basic needs and thereby reintegrate victims into productive community life. For justice to be served, we must offer victims of crime sufficient support to rebuild their lives.

As we think about how best to meet the needs of crime victims, we must examine the limitations of our current approach. Relying only on the traditional criminal justice process to provide justice to victims is fundamentally flawed for three reasons. First, few victims make it through the courthouse door. Most reports of crime do not result in arrests, fewer lead to prosecutions, and fewer still produce convictions. If we limit our conception of justice for victims to the outcomes of the criminal justice process, the vast majority of crime victims will have no experience of justice.

Second, even for those few crime victims whose offenders are prosecuted, participating in the criminal justice system in a role limited to serving as a witness for the prosecution and providing testimony as needed can be deeply troubling and unsatisfying. Many victims feel unfairly excluded from proceedings or disrespected by police, prosecutors and judges — people they had hoped would value their perspective. They experience a kind of institutionalized neglect, as though their crime-related needs and concerns are irrelevant. For many victims whose lives have been severely disrupted, who can no longer function as well at home, in school, or on the job, criminal prosecutions do little to restore their equilibrium.

Third, the traditional criminal justice process is ineffective at maximizing the safety and welfare of crime victims. When criminal justice officials focus exclusively on offender accountability and ignore the vulnerability of victims, they miss opportunities to prevent repeat victimization. Similarly, the failure to address the impact of crime on victims fuels many of the social problems that plague communities, and fails to interrupt patterns of violence and abuse that perpetuate criminal behavior.

Over the past generation, these criticisms have led to a number of significant reforms. Victim advocates have conducted training for criminal justice officials to encourage more compassionate treatment of victims. Police departments and prosecutors' offices have created victim assistance units designed to make victims' participation in the criminal justice system less burdensome. Legislative reforms gave victims rights to participate during critical stages of the criminal justice process.

These efforts have borne valuable fruit. Criminal justice officials are now better informed about crime victims' needs, and are more likely to treat victims respectfully. Victim advocates are able to keep victims apprised of the status of their cases, helping them to avoid unnecessary trips to court when there are postponements. Victims have attained legal rights to be informed about the status of their cases, to attend most court proceedings, and to participate at many stages of the criminal justice process, including conferring with prosecutors before plea bargains are reached, and offering victim impact statements at sentencing and parole hearings.

Even these advances, though, do not address the fundamental limitations of the traditional criminal justice process that remains offender-focused. For many victims, more respectful treatment by criminal justice officials, and expanded opportunities to have a voice in the process, still do not ensure either safety or justice.

Over the last thirty years, restorative justice initiatives have sought to address some of the shortcomings of the traditional criminal justice process by switching the focus from retribution and punishment to repairing the harm caused by crime. Restorative justice programs such as sentencing circles, victim-offender dialogues, and family group conferences stress the importance of righting the wrongs that have been done, and addressing the causes of the offending behavior.

Though restorative justice has made valuable contributions to our understanding of the impact of crime on individuals and communities, and the importance of addressing these personal harms, it is typically restricted to cases in which offenders have been apprehended, and the "restoration" it offers victims is usually limited to what those offenders and local community members can provide. Thus, like the traditional criminal justice process, restorative justice efforts fail to reach the vast majority of victims whose crime reports never result in arrests, and offer only a limited amount of assistance to those victims they do reach. Like the existing criminal justice process, restorative justice leaves us with an incomplete vision of how to promote safety and justice for victims.

During the past thirty years, we have also witnessed tremendous growth in victim services, both within criminal justice agencies and in community-based nonprofits, hospitals, and other social service organizations. Victim service providers assist millions of crime victims each year with a range of services including crisis intervention, supportive counseling, critical emergency assistance, and effective advocacy. All fifty states and the federal government have also developed victim compensation programs to reimburse eligible victims for crime-related expenses. Millions of dollars are dispensed each year to cover such costs as medical bills, lost wages, funeral expenses, and crime scene cleanup.

Nonetheless, many victims of crime cannot access the assistance they need. Service delivery remains uneven everywhere and almost nonexistent in some parts of the country. Compensation programs reach only a small portion of victims, and compensate them for only a fraction of their expenses. These shortcomings reflect a profound problem with our response to victims: as a nation, we have not yet embraced our societal obligation to help all victims of crime rebuild their lives. All too often, victim assistance is viewed as falling within the province of charity or a discretionary government program, rather than as an essential element of justice.

To achieve justice for victims of crime, several obstacles must be overcome. First, we must confront our reluctance to engage with victims' issues. As individuals, many of us do not want to associate with victims. We don't want to share a victim's experience or imagine that a similar crime could ever be committed against us. We raise questions that reveal personal fears, like, "What did she do to bring on this crime?" or, "Would I react the same way if it happened to me?" We believe we can immunize ourselves against crime by behaving or thinking differently from victims. We find it difficult to discuss crime with a victim, wanting to believe that it's private or that they would rather not discuss it. For many, it's much easier to talk to someone about a parent's death from cancer than to talk to someone about a parent's murder.

As Americans we are proud of our "can do" spirit and our belief in pulling ourselves up by our bootstraps, so when someone is victimized, we wonder what was wrong with them, and why they just can't get over it and move on with their lives. We must learn to listen to victims, to acknowledge the truth of their experience, and do everything we can to support them.

Media images create more obstacles. Victims highlighted by the media or by politicians are typically middle- or upper-class white people with no previous exposure to crime. Seen in isolation, these images are misleading because they don't focus on the people at greatest risk of experiencing crime in America—poor people of color living in crime-ridden communities. Our national discourse about victimization must acknowledge the complex reality of people who may experience crime on a regular basis.

Finally, two groups who could be natural allies in seeking Parallel Justice—criminal justice reformers and victim advocates—generally do not seek common ground in their work on behalf of offenders and victims. Criminal justice reformers (those working on issues such as stop and frisk policies, bail reform, indigent representation, sentencing, eyewitness testimony, court innovation, etc.) often worry that justice for victims could derail other criminal justice reform efforts. Victim advocates, on the other hand, often don't see the relevance of reforming a system that's essentially not about victims. But this is not a zero-sum game. Together, we must reframe justice issues to allow us to consider society's obligations to victims of crime, our separate commitments to offenders, and where those justice interests overlap.

This book looks at crime and justice from a victim's perspective. It does not present ideas for broader reform of the criminal justice system, nor does it address issues that are exclusively offender-oriented. Rather, it offers ideas for a parallel path to safety and justice, a new framework to better address the multiple, complex, and long-term needs of victims in the aftermath of crime.

Chapter 1 is an overview of the nature and extent of crime in America, focusing on the impact of crime on individuals, families, and communities. Chapter 2 describes current responses to victims, and discusses the major shortcomings of these responses. Chapter 3 establishes the guiding principles of Parallel Justice, and chapter 4 describes how those principles can be put into practice on the ground in communities. Finally, chapter 5 suggests strategies to begin to develop Parallel Justice initiatives.

1

Understanding the Impact of Crime

CRIME IS A DEFINING FEATURE OF LIFE IN AMERICA. Millions of Americans become victims of crime each year. Some move on with their lives with relative ease, while others experience continuing trauma without the services and support they need to repair the harm they suffered. Many crime victims lose their sense of confidence, feel isolated from other people, and experience a confusing and overwhelming range of emotions and ongoing psychological distress.[1]

The costs of crime are profound. Victimization takes an enormous toll on individual victims, their families and communities, and our nation as a whole. The emotional, physical, and financial impact of crime often leads to substance abuse, mental health problems, poor performance at school or work, and repeat victimization.

An essential foundation for the development of Parallel Justice is an understanding of the personal and communal impact of crime, as well as the inadequacy of the current societal response to victims. We need a new approach to providing support to crime victims. Parallel Justice is a universal response to all crime victims, offering a pathway to safety and justice, both within and outside the traditional criminal justice response. By addressing the costly personal and societal damage caused by crime, Parallel Justice creates wide-ranging benefits for individual victims and for society at large.

CRIME IN AMERICA

In 2007, Americans experienced 23 million violent and nonviolent crimes.[2] This translates into one crime almost every two seconds in communities across the country. About 1 in 4 of all crimes in the United States involves violence. More than 5 million violent crimes occurred in 2007, experienced by 21 out of every 1,000 people. The crime-specific numbers are staggering: in that year, there were over 4 million assaults, nearly 600,000 robberies, and nearly 250,000 sexual assaults. One-fifth of all violent crimes were committed by armed offenders.[3] And the most violent of violent crimes, homicide, occurred at a much higher rate in America than in any other industrialized nation. With 16,929 homicides in America in 2007,[4] homicide rates in this country are 3 to 5 times higher than in most of Europe.[5]

According to surveys or police reports, however, the great majority of crime in the United States involves nonviolent crime, such as larceny, household burglary, or motor vehicle theft. In 2007, there were almost 150 property crimes for every 1,000 people, or almost 18 million non-violent crime incidents overall. For every 1,000 Americans, there were 27 household burglaries, 8 motor vehicle thefts, and 111 other thefts.[6]

Identity theft, a type of property crime, is the fastest-growing crime in the United States. The Internet and the Information Age offer new opportunities to acquire and use personal identifying information to steal money, open fraudulent lines of credit, and create a new identity. Estimates vary on the extent of the problem, but a 2006 survey by the Federal Trade Commission estimated that over 8 million Americans had been victims of identity theft in the previous year.[7] In 2005, the National Crime Victimization Survey (NCVS) found that 6.4 million households—or 1 in every 20 households in America—had at least one household member who had been a victim of identity theft during the previous six months.[8]

The Unified Crime Reports (UCR) and the National Crime Victimization Survey (NCVS), the two major sources of crime data in the country, omit many categories of crime, including most reports of corporate or white-collar crime, so we do not have an accurate count of the victims of these crimes.

While crime strikes people of all races, ages, and walks of life, certain sectors of our society are more likely to be directly affected. Contrary to popular belief, elderly Americans are at relatively lower risk of being victims of violent crime, with rates of 2.5 violent crimes for every 1,000 people 65 and older, compared to about 129 violent crimes per 1,000 people for ages 12 to 24.[9] When compared with other age groups, however, people 65 or older are disproportionately affected by property crimes. Between 1993 and 2002, more than 9 in 10 crimes against the elderly were property crimes compared to 4 in 10 crimes against people age 12 to 24.[10]

Young people continue to be at the greatest risk of becoming victims of violent crime, especially young men of color. Teenagers and young adults ages 12 to 24 experienced violent crime at rates triple that for people ages 25 to 49.[11] A national survey of children between 10 and 16 years old revealed that more than half had been victims of violence. A quarter of these children had been victimized the previous year, 1 in 8 had been injured, and 1 in 100 needed medical attention as a result of the injury.[12]

Race and Class Differences

Violent crime is also more likely to affect people of color from poor communities. According to the NCVS, blacks experience the highest levels of violent victimization compared to other racial groups. For every 1,000 people in the following racial groups, 24 blacks, 19 Hispanics, 20 whites, and 11 people of other races experienced a violent crime in 2007.[13] A separate study of Native Americans revealed even higher rates of violence compared to other racial groups. Between 1992 and 2001, violent crime rates among Native Americans were more than double the crime rates of blacks and whites and over 4 times the crime rate of Asians.[14]

Focusing on homicide alone, the racial disparities are even starker.

In 2007, 49 percent of murder victims were black, although blacks represent only 13 percent of the population.[15] In 2006, the overall homicide rate for black victims in the United States was 20.27 per 100,000.[16] That same year, the national homicide rate was 5.38 per 100,000 people, and for whites it was 3.14 per 100, 000.[17] For African American teenagers and young adults in the United States, homicide is the leading cause of death.[18]

Inner city youth not only experience crime and violence at high rates, they also witness it at astounding levels. For instance, one survey of mothers conducted in an urban pediatric clinic found that 10 percent of their children between 1 and 5 years of age had witnessed a knifing or shooting, 18 percent had witnessed a beating, and 47 percent said they had heard gunshots in their neighborhood.[19] Another study found that among urban youth age 7–18, 43 percent had witnessed a murder.[20]

Family income is also an indicator of risk of crime. Households with annual incomes of less than $7,500 experienced significantly higher rates of burglary and theft compared to households earning more.[21]

As these data suggest, the consequences of crime are particularly acute in poor communities of color, where victims' needs are great, resources are scarce, and our failure to respond is that much more damaging to community life. The same crime-ridden communities where people are at great risk of victimization also have the highest rates of incarceration.[22] In fact, the lives of victims and offenders often overlap. Victims are likely to have a friend, neighbor, or family member who has been arrested, convicted, and incarcerated. Similarly, offenders from crime-ridden communities are likely to have been victims of crime as well.[23]

Crime Reporting Rates

According to the National Crime Victimization Survey, less than half of all crimes are reported to the police.[24] Among violent crimes in 2007, robbery was the most commonly reported: 66 percent of all robberies were brought to the attention of police. Only 42 percent of rape and sexual assaults were reported, and simple assault was the least likely to be reported to police (41 percent). Crimes involving female victims (47 percent) were only slightly more likely to be reported compared to crimes against males (45 percent).[25]

The reasons for not reporting a crime are often personal, sometimes determined by the circumstances of the crime or the resilience of the victim. Reasons most often attributed to victims of violent crime for not making a police report range from characterizing the crime as a "private/personal matter" or "not important enough" to that it had been "reported to some other official."[26]

A series of recent studies focusing on the experiences of domestic violence victims with the criminal justice system helps to shed some light on the complex calculus of victim reporting. Researchers found a connection between victim satisfaction with the criminal justice system in a prior case and a person's willingness to report future crimes. Women who had been victims before and chose not to report new incidents of abuse felt that the police actions in the prior case failed to keep them safe, and the prosecutor failed to seek serious enough charges against the offender. For these women, reporting the crime had failed to achieve any meaningful results.[27]

Widespread underreporting highlights a view, shared by many victims of crime, that the criminal justice system is not particularly effective in keeping them safe or in meeting their needs. If our society developed a response to crime that meets the fundamental needs of crime victims, one likely result is that more victims would be willing to report crimes to the police.[28]

REPEAT VICTIMIZATION

Just as research has now demonstrated that certain offenders can be identified as repeat offenders, and certain locations identified as crime-prone locations or "hot spots," so too the research on repeat victimization demonstrates that a known group of individuals—crime victims—are more likely, compared to individuals who have not been victims, to be victims again in the future. The phenomenon of repeat victimization offers a particularly persuasive argument for rethinking our response to crime. In fact, victims of many kinds of crime — including domestic violence, hate crimes, and most property crimes — are especially vulnerable during the period immediately following the crime.[29] The reality of repeat victimization underscores the importance of society's obligation to provide for the safety of victims of crime.

According to the research, repeat victimization accounts for a substantial portion of all crimes. In some crime categories, nearly half of all crime victims had recently been victims of the same crime.[30] According to analysis of data from the National Crime Victimization Survey, 49 percent of all sexual offenses, 43 percent of all assaults and threats, 33 percent of all burglaries, and 15 percent of thefts from persons in America are attributable to repeat victimization.[31]

The research on repeat victimization presents society with enormous crime prevention opportunities. Analysis of criminal history data and victimization surveys indicates that a small number of people and places account for a large percentage of all crimes. One survey reported that 4 percent of crime victims experience 44 percent of all crimes.[32] Finally, research documents that repeat offenses often occur soon after the first offense. In the period immediately after the crime, the victim faces a high risk of repeat victimization, followed by a sharp decline in the risk, until the victim has about the same victimization risk as people who have not experienced a previous crime.[33] A study of residential burglary in Tallahassee, Florida, found that 25 percent of repeats occurred within one week, and 51 percent within one month of the first burglary. Another study in Merseyside, England, found that 11 percent of repeat residential burglaries were committed within one week, and 33 percent within one month.[34] Effective interventions to prevent recurrence of these crimes could bring overall crime rates and victimization down substantially.

Research also reveals that the risk of repeat victimization varies by crime type:

Burglary – Data from the 1992 British Crime Survey indicate that 63 percent of the people who experienced property crime (defined as household burglaries and theft or damage inside or immediately outside the home) in a given year had already been victims of property crime during that same period.[35] Another study showed that over a six-year period, a quarter of the burglaries in one city took place in only 1.2 percent of the dwellings.[36] This increased rate and risk pertains both to businesses and private homes. An American study found that 36 percent of businesses burglarized were hit again within a year,[37] while a Canadian study found that homes burglarized are 4 times more likely to be burglarized as those not previously targeted.[38]

Sexual Assault – Compared to women with no history of sexual assault, the odds of experiencing a new assault over a two-year period doubled for women with one prior assault, quadrupled for women with two assaults, and elevated tenfold for women with three or more prior victimizations.[39] When samples are adjusted to include victims of child sexual abuse — a crime with a high level of repeat offenses — the numbers inflate to astounding levels. A woman who experienced sexual abuse as a child is 2 to 3 times more likely to be sexually assaulted later in life.[40] In general, sexual assault survivors are 35 times more likely to be repeat victims (of any type of crime) than non-victims.[41]

Domestic Violence – The crime perhaps most intuitively linked to incidences of repeat victimization is domestic violence. One study found that only 10 percent of all acts of domestic violence against women are isolated events, while 90 percent involve systematic, repeated, and escalating violence.[42] Another study reveals that over a 25-month period, 48 percent of calls to the police for domestic violence incidents came from only 10 percent of households reporting domestic violence.[43] That survey found that, after an initial police response to a domestic violence incident, 35 percent of households experienced another incident within only five weeks, while almost 20 percent of repeat offenses occurred within one day.[44]

Researchers identify two primary reasons for repeat victimization. First, some targets, either people or places, are more attractive to criminals because they are more vulnerable to crime. The location, physical condition, lighting, visibility, and even the landscaping may contribute to how vulnerable a business or home appears. Similarly, the extent to which people are isolated, or routinely travel in dangerous places, may increase their risk of being targeted for crime. If the reasons the target was vulnerable to crime remain the same after the crime occurs, the victim remains vulnerable and may be re-targeted by the same or other offenders.

The second reason for repeat victimization is that when people succeed in committing a crime, they often learn the best ways to do it again. They may gain information about a victim's possessions, work habits, or particular vulnerabilities, and learn how to access a targeted location or the placement of equipment or possessions in a home or business. This emboldens them to commit the same crime again. Whether someone is victimized repeatedly by different offenders or the same offender, research on repeat victimization reveals that failure to take protective steps to make a victim less vulnerable can increase the likelihood of repeat victimization.[45]

This research on repeat victimization supports the central tenet of Parallel Justice regarding our societal obligation to help crime victims. Because each crime involves a victim who faces an elevated probability of revictimization, each crime creates an obligation to intervene to prevent a recurrence. The imperative to keep victims safe thus coincides with society's interests in reducing the costs of crime and improving public safety.

Therefore, just as policymakers interested in reducing crime rates have focused on repeat offenders and "hot spots" to reduce crime, our society should focus on victims to help them be secure in the future. Such a strategy would not only demonstrate to victims that their government cares for their well-being, it would also reduce the overall rate of crime.

Consequences for Crime Victims

While statistics help create a sense of the magnitude of the phenomenon of crime in America, and paint a picture of the prevalence of crime in our lives, numbers alone do not reflect the harm done to the millions of people in crime's wake. Crime can have powerful, life-changing repercussions for victims' health, well-being, and financial stability. Mental illness, suicide, and substance abuse, for example, are far more common among crime victims than among the general public. The trauma of victimization can result in a range of reactions, from an immediate crisis response to longer-term emotional and psychological consequences.[46]

If our communal response to crime is to include justice for victims, we must understand their particular experience of crime and the harms they have suffered. To help victims rebuild their lives, we must understand what immediate and ongoing support victims need as they recover from the trauma of the crime.

Emotional Impact of Crime

In the immediate aftermath of crime, nearly all victims of serious crime experience fear, anger, confusion, frustration, guilt, shame, and grief, in varying degrees of intensity.[47] Exceptionally resilient victims move on with their lives easily. Others may cope with the emotional aftermath of their experience for weeks, months, and even years after the crime.

Accidents, natural disasters, illness, death of close relatives, loss of a job, and economic downturns can also result in deep and long-lasting trauma. But the experience of crime victims is different—the trauma and harm they suffer result from intentional acts of cruelty. The fact that another human being deliberately chose to take an unlawful action that harmed another person, or intentionally stole or damaged property, or even was indifferent to the harm he caused, changes the nature of the event and, in turn, the reactions to it. For example, the trauma that results from the loss of a child due to illness, or even an accidental drowning in a neighbor's pool, is not the same as the trauma experienced by parents of a murdered child. Similarly, the trauma experienced by a flood victim is not the same as the trauma experienced by a victim of arson.

This is not to say that the harm experienced by crime victims is greater, or that crime victims' pain is more severe. Rather the element of human cruelty or deliberate harm present in most crimes often results in a different set of reactions. Many crime victims develop a distrust of both intimates and strangers, experience a general sense of alienation from others, and tend to withdraw from many aspects of community life. Victims often feel that their experience is trivialized, or worse, not believed by others. Many feel shame, powerlessness, or tremendous insecurity after a crime. These reactions are common among victims of both violent and nonviolent crime—victims of assault as well as victims of fraud.

The severity of the trauma is an important determinant of the severity of its social and psychological effects. Among victims of violent crime, for instance, experiencing a rape, a life-threatening assault, or an injury from an attack is associated with an increased risk of post-traumatic stress disorder (PTSD).[48] First identified as a condition experienced by soldiers returning from war, PTSD is a set of reactions to a traumatic event characterized by recurring and often disabling symptoms of anxiety, flashbacks, avoidance, and hyperarousal.[49]

Researchers have found that victims of violent crime are at greater risk of developing PTSD than victims of non-criminal traumatic events such as natural disasters[50] (see figure 1.1). Nearly 40 percent of physical assault victims report PTSD symptoms at some point in their lives, and 18 percent report current PTSD (within the past six months). Rates of lifetime and current PTSD among rape victims are also high—32 percent and 12 percent respectively. Overall, 25 percent of victims of violent crime experience a lifetime risk of PTSD, and nearly 10 percent currently have PTSD. These levels of PTSD among crime victims stand in sharp contrast to the general population, in which the prevalence of PTSD is estimated to be only 3.6 percent.[51]

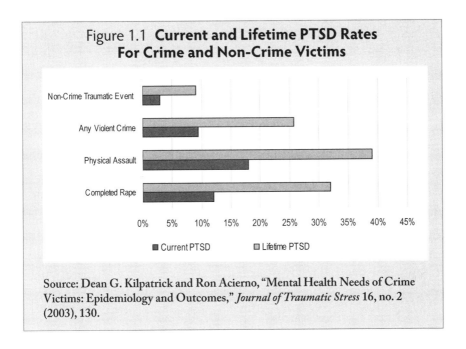

Figure 1.1 **Current and Lifetime PTSD Rates For Crime and Non-Crime Victims**

Source: Dean G. Kilpatrick and Ron Acierno, "Mental Health Needs of Crime Victims: Epidemiology and Outcomes," *Journal of Traumatic Stress* 16, no. 2 (2003), 130.

Victims of many kinds of crime are also more likely to experience symptoms of major depression. In a national study of adult women, 55 percent of aggravated assault victims met the diagnostic criteria for major depression.[52] Likewise, rape victims experienced major depression at higher rates compared to the general population: 30 percent of rape victims had had at least one major depressive episode in their lives, and 21 percent were currently coping with depression.[53] These rates are significantly higher than the general population, in which the estimated rate for experiencing a major depressive episode is 6.5 percent.[54]

In addition, research comparing battered women who have been abused on several occasions to women who have not been abused shows battered women are 5 times more likely to attempt suicide, 15 times more likely to abuse alcohol, 9 times more likely to abuse drugs, and 3 times more likely to be diagnosed as depressed or psychotic.[55] Similarly, children growing up in inner city neighborhoods surrounded by chronic violence are at greater risk for PTSD, smoking, depression, substance abuse, and engaging in violent behavior.[56]

Many victims abuse drugs or alcohol as a way of coping with their victimization. For instance, a study of adolescent girls found that those who experienced physical and/or sexual dating violence were more likely to exhibit problems with substance abuse such as heavy drinking, smoking, and increased risk of cocaine use.[57] A national study of women found a cyclical relationship between substance abuse and victimization — substance abuse leads to increased risk of assault, and assault leads to increased risk of substance abuse.[58]

Research points to another indicator of the long-term harmful effects of victimization, finding that victimization leads to delinquency and criminal behavior. A study by the National Council on Crime and Delinquency found that the single greatest factor in predicting criminal behavior on the part of teenagers was not teenage pregnancy, drug use, or truancy, but whether they had been victims of crime.[59] A report of the Office for Juvenile Justice and Delinquency Prevention reached a similar conclusion: violent victimization of juveniles is a critical risk factor, not only for future victimization, but also for subsequent violent offending.[60] Moreover, children who have been subject to abuse or neglect are also more likely to commit crimes as adults. Groundbreaking research by Cathy Spatz Widom provided the empirical evidence for what she refers to as the "cycle of violence," the intergenerational phenomenon that makes "abused and neglected children have significantly greater risk of becoming delinquents, criminals, and violent criminals."[61]

Just as we fail to fully appreciate the wide-ranging emotional impact of violent crime, our society also turns a blind eye to the complex and often painful aftermath of nonviolent crime. The consequences for victims of nonviolent crime often resemble the impact of violent crime.[62] Victims of crimes such as identity theft, healthcare fraud, investment or real estate fraud, or scams against the elderly report experiencing anger, depression, and increased levels of substance abuse. The intentional, deliberate harm inflicted on victims of property crime can also lead to alienation, insecurity, and emotional turmoil with long-term effects such as "divorce, estrangement from families, dependence on others, withdrawal from daily life, cessation of activities that victims found enjoyable or meaningful in the past and even placement in long-term care facilities."[63] Victims of identity theft have compared the emotional impact to "that felt by victims of violent crimes, including rape, violent assault, and repeated battering, with some reporting that they felt dirty, defiled, ashamed, embarrassed, and undeserving of assistance."[64] And although victims of nonviolent crime are less likely to experience PTSD than victims of violent crime,[65] one study of investment fraud showed that victims are "likely to suffer from major depressions, with a few experiencing suicidal ideation."[66] Clearly, if we are to mitigate the harmful consequences of crime, we must fully understand the impact of so-called "nonviolent crime," and we must address the needs of these victims as well as victims of violent crime.

Consequences for Communities

Although we tend to think of the damage caused by crime in terms of individual victims, communities also shoulder an enormous burden. The fear of strangers and general alienation from communal life experienced by crime victims is multiplied exponentially in communities experiencing high rates of crime and repeat victimization. Crimes against individuals ultimately erode the sense of safety and security of an entire community.[67]

High rates of crime and disorder are associated with higher rates of fear, neighborhood dissatisfaction, and a desire to leave the neighborhood. For example, one study found that individuals who had been the victim of a crime within one mile of home were more likely to move away from the neighborhood.[68] This can be disruptive for a community because the people who are most able to move are generally also those who provide the human and social capital that is essential to the growth of the community.[69] This selective out-migration is often coupled with selective in-migration as families and individuals with fewer resources move into high-crime neighborhoods. Businesses also tend to leave high-crime communities, forcing residents to do their shopping outside their neighborhood, further eroding a community's resources and its sense of cohesiveness[70] (see table 1.1).

Table 1.1 **Consequences of Crime**	
INDIVIDUAL	**SOCIETAL**
Life course disruption	Victim assistance, social services costs
Lost days at work or school	Decreased productivity
Property damage or loss	Devalued or unusable resources
Medical and mental health problems	Healthcare costs
Drug and alcohol abuse	Anti-social behavior, treatment costs
Participation in criminal justice process	Criminal justice costs
Diminished quality of life	Community instability, disorder
Fear of crime	Social alienation
Repeat victimization and/or subsequent criminal behavior	More crime

The research on the personal, community, and societal consequences of crime makes a powerful case for supporting individual crime victims as they cope with crime's many ripple effects. Failure to mitigate these harms means that victims are left to fend for themselves, and the damage to both individuals and communities is left unattended. By contrast, providing meaningful assistance to crime victims reduces alienation, ameliorates emotional and psychological stress, reduces the incidence of substance abuse, depression, and mental illness associated with crime, and makes it far less likely that victims of crime will be re-victimized or engage in subsequent criminal behavior.

One study of battered women in Michigan offers a particularly compelling illustration of the value of assisting victims to reconnect with supportive social networks. In a two-year random-assignment experiment testing the impact of free short-term advocacy services for battered women as they left a shelter, researchers found that those who received support to access both community resources and social services reported not only a higher quality of life, but also significantly less abuse.[71] This suggests that addressing crime victims' needs comprehensively would go a long way toward enhancing individual and community safety and ultimately repairing the fabric of communities torn apart by crime.

COSTS OF CRIME

On both individual and societal levels, crime exacts a high price in terms of the cost of healthcare, social services, and lost productivity. Crime victims frequently must take off work to attend court hearings. Some are unable to continue in their current jobs due to crime-related physical injuries or because they are still coping with depression or anxiety. Others cannot absorb the costs of healthcare or lost property or damage to their homes or cars.

Financial Impact of Crime on Victims

Crime victims must cope with financial losses from damaged or stolen property, medical and mental health expenses, and missed workdays. Over 18 million violent and nonviolent crime victimizations—or 8 out of 10 victimizations—resulted in economic losses in 2005.[72] A further breakdown shows a disproportionate financial burden on victims of nonviolent crimes: 19 percent of the 5.1 million violent crimes and 96 percent of the 18 million nonviolent crimes produced out-of-pocket financial losses for the victims.[73] Victims of financial crime have lost their homes, "life savings, pensions, children's college funds, and inheritances. Because some victims have gone into debt, declared bankruptcy, or had bank accounts frozen or closed, they can no longer pay bills and conduct business, are pursued by collection agencies, sued, or even charged criminally for unknowingly depositing and drawing on counterfeit checks."[74]

According to one national study, victims of intimate partner violence, including rape, physical assault, and stalking, experience substantial lost time in employment and household work. Annually, domestic violence victims miss nearly 8 million days of paid work because of the violence in their lives—equal to over 32,000 full-time jobs. This violence also results in an annual loss of over 5 million days of household work.[75]

A survey by the Federal Trade Commission (FTC) found that identity theft victims spend an average of 30 hours a year resolving problems associated with misuse of their personal information. Over a one-year period, Americans spent nearly 300 million hours resolving problems associated with identity theft.[76] The total annual cost of identity theft in the United States in 2005 was $15.6 billion.[77]

Financial Burden of Crime on Society

Aggregating the costs of crime presents a sobering picture of the financial burden on society. According to a study by the National Institute of Justice (NIJ), crime is associated with an estimated $105 billion in medical expenses, lost earnings, and costs for victim services.[78] Factoring in intangible costs such as pain and suffering and a diminished quality of life brings the total estimated cost of crime in America to $450 billion annually.[79] A report by the Centers for Disease Control and Prevention estimates that the health-related costs alone of intimate partner violence exceed $5.8 billion annually, nearly $4.1 billion of which is for direct medical and mental healthcare services.[80]

The costs associated with a single victimization are equally sobering. The NIJ report found that a single homicide is estimated to cost society nearly $3 million; a rape results in $87,000 in economic and non-economic losses, and a household burglary, on average, creates $1,400 in losses[81] (see table 1.2).

Table 1.2 **Estimated Costs of Crime, 1996**	
Type of Crime	**Total Per Crime Costs**
Homicide	$2,940,000
Rape / Sexual Assault	87,000
Assault	
with injury	24,000
without injury	2,000
Robbery	
with injury	19,000
without injury	2,000
Property Crime	
Motor vehicle theft	$3,700
Household burglary	1,400
Theft	370

These estimates include three categories of costs: 1) out-of-pocket expenses such as medical bills and property loss; 2) reduced productivity at home, work, and school; and 3) non-economic losses such as increased fear, pain and suffering, and diminished quality of life. These three categories also provide a useful framework for understanding the potential positive impact of helping victims rebuild their lives more effectively. If we helped crime victims establish healthy, communal lives, we would mitigate their out-of-pocket financial losses. Similarly, appropriate assistance would increase victims' productivity at work or in school. Finally, responding to the full range of victims' needs would also ameliorate non-economic losses, the intangible effects of crime, such as increased fear, alienation, suffering, and diminished quality of life. These effects of crime are particularly corrosive because they weaken societal bonds and increase the isolation of crime victims. A just response to victims would place a high priority on addressing all of these emotional, physical, and financial effects of crime.

Conclusion

Crime affects millions of Americans each year, a significant portion of whom remain psychologically, physically, and financially unstable afterward. Victims experience a wide variety of negative consequences, including physical and mental illness, economic losses, diminished self-confidence, and loss of trust in others. Although it is rarely recognized, each new victim also faces an elevated risk of being victimized again, creating a cycle of new crimes and new harms. Moreover, victims of certain crimes are themselves at greater risk of engaging in criminal behavior.

Each crime creates ripple effects throughout the lives of individual victims, their families, and their communities. At a community level, high rates of crime translate into elevated levels of fear and loss of social cohesion. Crime causes businesses and residents alike to leave dangerous neighborhoods in search of safer ones. Added to these harms experienced by individuals and communities are the significant financial costs of crime borne by employers, the social-service support systems, and the economy.

Repairing the harm caused by crime requires focusing on victims' safety and addressing the range of emotional, physical, and financial problems that too often leave victims unable to lead healthy and productive lives. If we respond to individuals' crime-related needs, as envisioned in the Parallel Justice framework, we are more likely to have a positive impact on many of the harmful byproducts of crime — the health problems, the substance abuse, the poor academic and job performance, the emotional and financial instability, the homelessness, and criminal behavior—often associated with victimization. Finally, a Parallel Justice response to crime will mitigate the debilitating sense of social isolation and the profound lack of trust and confidence in our government experienced by many victims of crime.

⊣ | | | ⊢

2

Assessing Our Current
Response to Victims of Crime

OVER THE PAST FORTY YEARS, our country has witnessed remarkable innovations designed to improve the way we respond to victims of crime. Troubled by the grim statistics about the extent of crime in America, and moved by the harms that victims have suffered, a generation of reformers came to view the agencies of the criminal justice system as unresponsive to the needs of victims. These reformers advocated for new policies and practices that help victims regain their health, cope with their losses, and return to their status as productive members of society. Waves of innovation and advocacy transformed the way society thinks about the impact of crime and responds to those victimized by it.

Before developing the concept of Parallel Justice, we must first assess the effectiveness of reforms that were launched over the past four decades. These reforms fall under two broad headings: 1) those designed to repair the harm caused by crime; and 2) those designed to improve the experiences of crime victims as they participate in the criminal justice process.

The first category covers a broad range of services to crime victims, including many new services that did not exist before, such as rape hotlines, shelters for victims of domestic violence, child advocacy centers, and support groups for families of homicide victims. One of the most widespread initiatives involved creation of victim compensation programs that provide reimbursement for certain expenses victims incur as a result of crime.

The second category includes a variety of innovations designed to change the relationship between victims and the formal criminal justice process. Beginning in the early 1970s, jurisdictions around the country embraced efforts to increase victim participation in court proceedings. At the same time, a new set of legal rights was created for crime victims, some embedded in state constitutions, others codified in state and federal legislation. These new rights provide crime victims with opportunities to receive information, be consulted, and participate in various stages of the criminal justice process. Criminal justice reformers have also tested new ways of resolving criminal disputes, such as mediation, and more recently, restorative justice, both of which envision different, more participatory roles for crime victims.

The past four decades have witnessed an impressive array of new ideas to address the needs of crime victims. It's important, however, that we recognize both the progress we have made and the limits of these efforts. The following discussion examines these innovations, assessing first the initiatives that address the harms of crime, and then those that seek to improve the experiences of victims in the criminal justice process. The overarching question is whether these efforts meet victims' needs by keeping them safe and providing them sufficient support. The answer to this question underscores the need for a fundamentally different approach to how we conceptualize justice for victims of crime.

EFFORTS TO REPAIR THE HARM

Now, almost forty years into the victims' movement, the breadth of services available to victims of crime stands in stark contrast to the paucity of resources available when it began. Principally due to the efforts of both feminist and victim advocacy organizations, great progress has been made in helping to ease the trauma victims have suffered.

Victim Compensation

One of the most significant reform initiatives of the 1960s was the development of state-level programs offering eligible victims financial compensation for certain out-of-pocket expenses. Victim compensation is one of the most important, tangible demonstrations of a societal response. Reimbursing victims for crime-related expenses is a concrete way for the government to help victims endure the cost of crime. Clearly, these funds make a real difference in the lives of crime victims, and the existence of a network of compensation programs represents a significant accomplishment of the victim advocates of a previous generation.

California established the first victim compensation program in 1965, followed by New York, Hawaii, Massachusetts, Maryland, and the Virgin Islands.[1] These initiatives spread rapidly throughout the country after 1984 when the federal government passed the Victims of Crime Act (VOCA), which supports compensation programs in all fifty states and the District of Columbia.[2]

The number of compensation claims filed and awarded has grown since the program began. In 1998, states paid a total of 117,486 claims to crime victims, totaling $265,522,894.[3] In 2008, state victim compensation programs across the country paid a total of 151,643 claims to victims, totaling $431,904,585.[4]

Unfortunately, however, victim compensation programs exclude most victims. The original Victims of Crime Act limited eligibility to victims of violent crimes. In 2001, Congress modified these restrictions and expanded eligibility to victims of financial crimes, though the new guidelines specified that states should still give priority to victims of violent crime.[5] As a result, state compensation programs that reimburse homicide survivors or assault victims for crime-related expenses such as lost wages, transportation to and from court, or psychological counseling typically do not compensate victims of burglary, fraud, or identity theft for similar losses. Because three-fourths of victims of crime in America experience financial or property crime, these restrictions, whether in the form of explicit policies or just common practices, have the effect of excluding millions of victims every year.

States also limit the amount of coverage for economic losses sustained through violent crime. Most state programs specify a short list of kinds of losses that will be covered, and do not invite victims to seek compensation for any crime-related expense. Some states allow victims to apply for a non-enumerated expense, but generally victims don't know they can do so. In addition, even though states have the discretion to reimburse victims for non-economic losses such as pain and suffering, only two states, Hawaii and Tennessee, do.[6]

Compounding these eligibility problems, most states place time limits on filing for compensation, which unnecessarily restricts the number of victims that can be compensated. Some victims don't hear about compensation until long after the crime. Some are too distraught or too focused on other priorities to fill out the application in time. Still others have crime-related expenses that continue long past the filing deadline.[7] According to an Urban Institute study, even after taking into account other sources of compensation, two-thirds of the respondents in a claimant survey reported that they sustained unrecovered losses with an average loss of $5,762."[8] Thus, impressive gains notwithstanding, most victims are still left without adequate financial assistance as they try to repair the harms caused by crime.

The amount of compensation available for crime victims is further limited for reasons that can be traced to the origins of the state compensation programs: they are run by state governments, and supported by both the states and the federal government. Federal support comes from the Crime Victims Fund (the Fund) created by VOCA, and funded through fines and penalties collected from people convicted of federal crimes. Since its creation, the Fund has never received any federal tax revenue, only offender fines and penalties.

Each state receives annual federal funding equal to 60 percent of its compensation awards from the previous year.[9] States must cover the remainder of the costs of their programs. Most states also generate funding for compensation programs from offender fines; only six states use a combination of tax revenue and offender fines, and seven states rely entirely on tax revenue for their portion of the funding.[10]

Limiting federal and most of state funding to offender fines has understandable popular appeal because it is regarded as a form of indirect restitution. On balance, however, it is problematic to rely exclusively on this method of funding compensation for crime victims, for two primary reasons. First, the amount of money in the Crime Victims Fund fluctuates from year to year according to the unpredictable outcomes of criminal trials. Our nation's commitment to victims should not ebb and flow with the identification and successful prosecution of criminals. Second, we should not rely exclusively on offenders to meet victims' needs. Restricting funding resources only to offender fines means that society as a whole has not been asked to demonstrate a commitment to what should be a critical social priority, one that could be supported through tax dollars, licensing fees, or any other mechanism that generates a larger and broader base of support.

Victim Services

The same generation that witnessed the creation of compensation programs saw major improvements in the social service, healthcare, and private sector responses to crime victims. For instance, in the mid-1970s only a handful of shelters existed to help battered women in the United States. In 2009, the National Center for Victims of Crime listed over 2000 shelters for victims of domestic violence in its Helpline database. In the healthcare arena, it is now required that emergency personnel be trained to recognize and respond to underlying problems consistent with intentional injuries. As a result, doctors and nurses in emergency rooms are now more likely to recognize gang members, battered women, and abused children, not just gunshot wounds, black eyes, and broken arms.

Other sectors of government services have also seen significant reform. Several jurisdictions give public housing priority to victims of domestic violence. Many police agencies created special victims units, and trained their employees to respond to victims with greater sensitivity. Many prosecutors, judges, probation officers, and corrections professionals have adopted policies and launched training programs designed to improve interactions with crime victims.

Reforms to improve our response to crime victims have not been limited to the public sector. Businesses have also developed a greater understanding of the impact crime has on individual employees' health and safety, and, ultimately, on productivity. Accordingly, many large corporations have begun to provide assistance to employees coping with crime-related emergencies. Recognizing the high cost of losing seasoned employees to crime, a few businesses have even created company-wide training programs for employees to reduce their vulnerability to crime.

In the best of circumstances, service providers, whether in the public or private sector, offer a wide variety of resources to victims of crime. These include practical assistance, such as changing locks, providing food, clothing, transportation, and shelter—services that can make an immediate difference in the lives of victims and reduce the possibility of repeat victimization. But they also include services that will have long-lasting beneficial effects such as employment counseling, housing, and long-term support groups and counseling. A generation ago, many of these services did not exist, and the availability of these tangible supports represents enormous progress in the effort to repair the harm caused by crime.

Despite this progress, however, our efforts to help victims remain insufficient in several ways. First, most victim services are geared to, and available for, adult victims of violent crime. Though teenagers and young adults are far more likely than any other age group to become victims of violent crime,[11] they have the fewest services available to them. Children are highly vulnerable to crime. In a national survey of children from 2 to 17 years old, more than half had experienced an assault the previous year, more than 1 in 8 had experienced maltreatment, and 1 in 12 had experienced a sexual victimization. More than

1 in 4 had experienced a property crime such as theft or vandalism. More than 1 in 3 had witnessed violence or experienced another kind of indirect victimization. Only 29 percent had experienced no victimization at all within the previous year. It is particularly troubling that the mean number of victimizations for a child or youth was three. A child with one victimization had a 69 percent chance of experiencing another within a year.[12] Given the importance of promoting healing and interrupting destructive patterns of behavior as soon as possible, both to avoid repeat victimization and to decrease the risk of juvenile delinquency and adult criminal behavior, our failure to respond appropriately to young victims of crime is particularly unfortunate.[13]

A second category of victims—people who suffer the trauma of economic loss through fraud, identity theft, burglary, or other property crime—also have great difficulty finding appropriate services. Three-fourths of crime victims in America experience financial or nonviolent crimes.[14] Most victim services, however, are limited to victims of violent crime, either by program design or as a result of government funding restrictions.[15] Elderly people who lose their life savings through fraud experience many of the same types of trauma as victims of violent crime. In fact, victims of burglary, extortion, or vandalism may also experience physical, emotional, and financial problems as a result of the crimes committed against them. They all deserve support to help them get back on track.

Victim services are insufficient in another critical respect: many victims face enormous challenges accessing whatever resources and services may be available. Some live in areas with few victim services, such as rural parts of the country, or in high-crime neighborhoods. Some have difficulty finding services that are offered after normal working hours. Others have to overcome barriers of language or physical or mental disabilities. For some crime victims, particularly ethnic, racial, and sexual minorities, it can be overwhelming to try to find culturally appropriate resources and services. One national study of victim assistance found that, especially in urban areas, victims of color have significantly more unaddressed needs than white victims of crime have. Unaddressed needs included tangible, concrete forms of assistance as well as information and advocacy.[16]

Another reason victims have difficulty accessing resources is that services are offered to limited categories of victims rather than to any victim as needed. For example, a range of emergency housing options is available to battered women, but fewer options exist for battered men, and even fewer for other crime victims who also fear for their safety in their own homes. Hospitals have created special services for victims of sexual assault to ensure that they are examined with sensitivity and to help them recover from the trauma they have experienced, but, except for a handful of programs, similar services have not been developed for men who have been raped, or for victims of other crimes who could benefit from them, such as victims of other types of assault.

Many victims feel invisible. Victims of crimes that take place in prisons, nursing homes, mental health facilities, homeless shelters, in the military, or on college campuses often have great difficulty convincing authorities that a crime occurred, and even more difficulty accessing assistance. Their experiences are more likely to be categorized as violations of procedures, maltreatment, abuses of authority, or even neglect, rather than criminal behavior. People in these environments experience a range of crimes, yet they rarely receive acknowledgment that what happened to them was against the law. As a result, crime victim services are rarely delivered inside these institutions.

Moreover, while an impressive array of victim services has developed—including crisis intervention, emergency assistance such as food, clothing, and shelter, individual and group counseling, and advocacy through the criminal justice, healthcare, and public assistance systems—many of the critical challenges victims face remain unaddressed. In the aftermath of crime, victims' lives often change dramatically. They may suddenly need daycare, employment training, short- or long-term psychotherapy, low-interest loans, home repair or relocation, or substance abuse treatment. Most victim service providers are unable to access such resources for their clients.

Finally, addressing victims' needs requires creativity. For example, an assault victim may need plastic surgery to repair disfigurement. A mugging victim may need an escort or special transportation to feel safe enough to do errands or be out at night. A family whose home has been burglarized may need someone to take care of children who are now too afraid to be home alone after school. Someone who has lost a partner or spouse to murder may need the assistance of a financial planner to think through a future without the other's income. Someone injured by a sexual assault may need help with cooking, taking care of pets, and other household chores while recovering. A student whose laptop computer has been stolen may need help replacing it. Most victim advocates are not equipped to address these kinds of problems.

Our approach to helping victims rebuild their lives is too often circumscribed by the status of preexisting victim services in a given community, and is not sufficiently driven by individual victim's actual needs. Often victim service providers are too overwhelmed with clients to be able to individualize services to that extent, especially since the kind of assistance they can offer is usually too restricted by funders' guidelines to allow such flexibility. Accordingly, service providers often ask only about victims' needs that would fit into preexisting services, rather than exploring more broadly what might help them move on with their lives and connecting them to the best options available.

Current efforts to provide resources and services to victims of crime have also not been sufficiently guided by research. Four examples are particularly noteworthy. First, one of the most significant crime-related discoveries of the last fifty years is that victims of many crimes become more vulnerable to another instance of the same crime for a period of time, until their risk returns to the same level as those who have not been victimized. Although the phenomenon of repeat victimization is well documented, victim advocates have adapted their services to address it only in certain circumstances.[17] Advocates develop safety plans with victims of domestic violence and stalking, and to a lesser degree with victims of sexual assault, but far less frequently with victims of other crimes. In fact, while it is contradicted by the research on repeat victimization, victim advocates working with victims of other crimes too often assure victims that lightning rarely strikes twice and they are safe.

Second, only a handful of cities and states have conducted their own victimization surveys to gather information about the experiences of crime victims in their jurisdiction. Without regularly interviewing a random sample of victims, it is impossible to determine what local victims needed in the aftermath of crime, what assistance they were able to access, and what concerns remained. Without local data, resources and services cannot be tailored to meet the specific needs of local victims.

Third, the victim services field has not yet developed a mature body of research evidence to determine the effectiveness of many of the services being offered. Few interventions are rigorously evaluated, and funders typically do not provide enough resources to carry out such evaluations. Some programs that have been evaluated and found to be of minimal value are still promoted to victims without sufficient cautionary warnings. A particularly troubling example involves certain models of court-mandated batterers' programs, which have been found to have little or no effect on reducing the level of intimate partner violence,[18] but which nonetheless are still considered appropriate placements for many men who abuse their partners. While policymakers and service providers may have other goals for these programs, such as increasing offender accountability, research tells us that many battered women stay with or return to men who have beaten them, in large part because they believe these programs will make the batterers less violent.[19] This awareness creates an added responsibility for victim advocates to caution their clients about the limited efficacy of such programs and the actual risks involved in returning to or staying with violent partners. More research is needed to determine what kinds of responses reduce levels of violence, and for which categories of batterers.

Finally, though the link between victimization and later delinquent and criminal behavior is well documented, very few corrections, probation, or parole departments have adapted their work to address the prior victimization of the people they supervise. In addition to education and job-skills programs, victim services may provide an important ingredient to successful reintegration of offenders. Research is needed to determine whether focusing on their past victimization could not only promote better mental health and greater productivity among offenders, but also help prevent recidivism.

This review of the past generation of reforms produces a mixed assessment. Clearly, hundreds of thousands of crime victims have benefited from the availability of services, and their lives have been improved as a result. These services, however, exclude large numbers of victims. The availability of services is highly uneven. In many parts of the country, victim services are nonexistent. These significant shortcomings underscore the conclusion that, as a nation, we have not yet embraced our obligation to help victims of crime rebuild their lives. In the future, the goals of keeping victims safe, preventing repeat victimization, and making sure that all victims have access to sufficient resources to become healthy and productive members of society, must be seen as essential elements of justice.

IMPROVING VICTIMS' EXPERIENCES IN THE CRIMINAL JUSTICE PROCESS

Reformers seeking to improve society's response to crime victims have also focused a substantial amount of attention on the workings of the criminal justice system. Over the same period of time that witnessed the growth of victim services and victim advocacy, the American public, acting through its elected officials, has significantly increased its reliance on the workings of the police, prosecutors, courts, and prisons as the preferred response to crime. Thus, just as the public believes that the traditional criminal justice system is the best response to crime, so too many victim advocates, and others who invoked victims' best interests, turned to the justice system as the place to find justice for victims of crime.

Seeking justice for victims in the traditional criminal justice process, though understandable, only leads to limited success. First, few crime victims ever see the inside of a courthouse. The vast majority do not end up in court because their reports are not investigated, the people who committed the crimes are not arrested or charged, or prosecutors decide not to proceed. Nationally, of the offenses reported to the police, only a small percentage result in convictions.[20] Therefore, to the extent reformers look to the criminal justice system to improve society's response to victims, any improvements will benefit only a small percentage of victims.

Second, the criminal justice system is notoriously inhospitable to crime victims, whose experiences are often frustrating, disappointing, or, at worst, harmful. Instead of receiving compassion and understanding from criminal justice professionals, many victims encounter insensitive, victim-blaming responses that compound their trauma. Even when victims do not experience poor treatment by the system, they often feel that the process doesn't offer any of the resources or services they need. The criminal justice system is, after all, focused on prosecuting offenders and adjudicating their crimes. With limited exceptions, it's not designed to address the impact of these crimes.

A number of studies confirm that most victims' experiences in the criminal justice system are unsatisfying. One study on victim noncooperation with the justice system revealed that the treatment victims receive is almost inevitably alienating.[21] A 1999 survey of crime victims in nine states revealed extensive dissatisfaction with the way cases were handled. According to this survey, the problem of dissatisfaction was not strictly related to the outcome in the criminal case. In fact, when asked to name the least satisfying aspect of their court experience, the same percentage of victims named poor communication with criminal justice agencies as mentioned lenient sentencing.[22]

A recent National Institute of Justice study of the experiences of domestic violence victims highlights a particularly troubling consequence of this disconnect: even though these victims had turned to the criminal justice system for help, they had become so dissatisfied with their treatment that they said they were less likely to call the police the next time they experienced a crime.[23] Andrew Karmen, a leading criminologist, captured the frustration of many crime victims when he stated, "The criminal justice system does not measure up to expectations. It fails to deliver on what it promises. It does not meet the needs and wants of victims as its 'clients' or 'consumers' of its services."[24]

Third, it is particularly noteworthy that agencies of the criminal justice system do not accept preventing repeat victimization as part of their mission. While there are certainly exceptions in which officials respond to victims' safety concerns by taking action to prevent further harm, these efforts are highly disproportionate to the risks victims face.

Notwithstanding the limited reach of the justice process and the seemingly insuperable obstacles to systemic change, a generation of victim advocates has sought, with considerable success, to improve the experiences of crime victims in the nation's courts. The following sections focus on three such efforts: a federally funded initiative to increase the participation of victims in court proceedings; an extraordinary national campaign to secure new rights for victims of crime; and a recent movement to embrace the philosophy of restorative justice, an alternative way to handle criminal disputes. These narratives lead to similar conclusions — that even though system reform is difficult, new policies and practices can be introduced that improve the experience of victims in the criminal justice process. Without more fundamentally different approaches, however, victims continue to feel that their needs and concerns are largely irrelevant to the justice process.

Increasing Victim Participation In the Criminal Justice Process

In the early 1970s, a number of American criminal justice officials expressed serious concerns about the low level of participation by victims and witnesses in the criminal justice system. In 1973, the U.S. Department of Justice published the first national victimization survey, which showed, for the first time, that half of all crime victims did not report their crimes to the police.[25] Other research showed that many victims did not come to court to participate in criminal prosecutions.[26] The implication was clear: criminals were going free, and cases were being lost, because witnesses were not participating.

Government interest in a more effective system of detecting, solving, and prosecuting crimes coincided with the rallying cry of a nascent victim advocacy movement seeking greater respect for victims, more attention to their needs, and greater accountability of offenders through restitution. These two interests coalesced to promote the policy goal of increasing victim participation in the justice system. Police and prosecutors supported these efforts because they knew: "no witness, no justice." Advocates supported victim participation because they believed it was not only good for victims' emotional well-being, but also made for better, more informed decision-making by prosecutors and judges. With this strong support from a variety of influential voices, a national effort was launched to increase victim participation in the criminal justice system.

Typically, these initiatives were based in prosecutors' offices where protocols were developed to notify victims about upcoming court dates, answer questions about the court process, and explain how a trial might proceed. At the heart of these reforms was the notion that victims who had more information about how the system functioned would be more likely to serve as witnesses, and therefore more prosecutions would be successful. Accordingly, the victim assistance efforts undertaken by the early prosecutor-based projects were not designed to help victims as much as they were to bolster prosecutions.

While most of these programs focused on providing information to victims in order to improve their participation rates, other initiatives were designed to improve participation by making the whole court process less burdensome for victims. The story of the Victim/Witness Assistance Project, or VWAP, an initiative of the Vera Institute of Justice in the early 1970s, highlights important lessons from these programs. VWAP was a large-scale project in Brooklyn, New York, funded by the federal government as a response to the startling findings regarding victim non-reporting from the first victimization study. One million dollars was invested to make it easier for victims to come to court. The project built a daycare center so victims could drop their children off while going to court, offered counseling to those suffering from trauma, provided assistance with filing for victim compensation, notified all victims and witnesses of their court dates by phone and computer-generated letters, and developed a program to allow victims and witnesses to stay at work on court dates, calling them only if their testimony was actually needed. While victims appreciated the services, and did find the process less burdensome, the evaluation found that the rate of appearances in court was nearly the same as before the program started.[27]

The Vera Institute of Justice took these disappointing research findings and developed two new initiatives: one providing mediation in felony cases involving parties who knew each other before the criminal incident, and one offering victim advocates who would appear in court to ensure that the victim was heard when appropriate. These initiatives, both creating more meaningful roles for victims, were somewhat more successful. When victims were given the option of mediation, a less formal process that encourages victims' participation and results in more individualized outcomes tailored to their needs, victims' satisfaction levels were higher. Victims who had gone through mediation tended to feel that the process was fairer, and the outcomes more satisfactory, than those who went through the traditional court process.[28]

The second initiative, the Victim Involvement Project (VIP), was designed to evaluate the impact of "a systematic effort to communicate the concerns of individual victims to officials in Brooklyn Criminal Court, one of the busiest courts in the nation."[29] One expectation was that if victims felt their views were considered, they would be more satisfied with the criminal justice process. The research design involved placing victim advocates in the District Attorney's Office for several purposes: They were to assist victims in a variety of ways including expediting the return of vouchered property, seeking employers' permission for victims to take time off, and explaining the court process. Advocates were also supposed to communicate victims' views to prosecutors.[30]

The evaluators found that, in many respects, advocates were able to make the process less burdensome for victims.[31] They also found, however, that the close working relationship the advocates developed with the prosecutor created significant role conflict, with advocates tending to modify victims' wishes to reflect typical outcomes rather than presenting the victims' actual views to the prosecutor.[32] Even when victims' views were presented to prosecutors, they were frequently not made known to the court, and, according to the evaluators, probably not considered by the prosecutors in fashioning their own positions in cases.[33] The study offered two explanations for this troubling lack of communication. First, individual prosecutors understandably feel constrained by the policies of their office, and therefore tend not to exercise a great deal of discretion when handling cases. Second, the enormous system-wide pressures to dispose of cases as quickly as possible serve as strong disincentives to take any action that might slow the wheels of justice.[34]

It is perhaps not surprising then that victims who participated in the Victim Involvement Project were no more satisfied with the process or the outcome than those who didn't participate. According to the evaluation, "One victim summed it up well when she said that although VIP staff members were 'wonderful,' she did not think that they 'really had the power to do anything.'"[35]

Providing system-based victim support services alone will not change the deeply entrenched culture and the primary focus of the criminal justice system. Furthermore, criminal justice agencies do not have the capacity or the mandate to address many of the problems victims face. Without a separate process for victims to express their needs and concerns directly to an authority who can respond to them, victims will continue to be disappointed in the criminal justice process, and their participation is unlikely to increase.

Securing Legal Rights
In the Criminal Justice Process

One of the most remarkable developments in criminal justice over the past generation has been the creation of a body of policies, statutes, and constitutional rights that have redefined the relationship of crime victims to the criminal justice process. In many ways, these reforms were responsive to the same realities documented in the empirical research on the victim assistance projects discussed above — namely, that the criminal justice system does not welcome the participation of crime victims.

The underlying objective of the victims' rights reform agenda has been to hold government accountable to a group of citizens who have been excluded from a vital set of government functions. Reformers have argued that because the criminal justice process was inhospitable to victims' participation, it was necessary to create a set of legal rights that would secure a place at the justice table for victims of crime. Because prosecutors, courts, corrections departments, and parole agencies were viewed as systematically excluding victims from critical proceedings, and because they were not considering victims' needs and concerns in their decision-making, state and federal legislatures would have to step in to ensure that, at critical points, victims would be welcome and their perspectives considered during certain deliberations. Finally, reformers asserted, because these agencies did not routinely tell crime victims about decisions that might affect them, laws should be enacted and state constitutions amended to require that they provide this information.

These arguments have been enormously successful. Over a twenty-year period, every state passed some version of a "victims' bill of rights." The federal government also enacted considerable legislation creating rights for victims,[36] and different versions of a victims' rights amendment to the United States Constitution have been proposed and introduced in Congress. This legal revolution has been one of the most important accomplishments of a generation of victim advocates. Most of the rights enacted during this period can be divided into three categories: the right to be informed, the right to be present, and the right to be heard.

THE RIGHT TO BE INFORMED

For many victims, the most fundamental right is the right to information.[37] There are two types of information that are of interest to victims. First, victims need to know what legal rights they have if they are to exercise them. For example, victims will not necessarily offer a victim impact statement before sentencing unless they know they have a right to do so. Similarly, they may not offer to explain why they believe incarceration is or is not still appropriate during a parole hearing, unless they know they have a legal right to do so. All fifty states have given victims rights to some information. Most states give victims the right to be informed of their rights. Many have also given victims a right to general information about local victim services, victim compensation and the criminal justice process.[38]

Second, victims are also interested in specific information about their cases, including the dates and times of criminal justice proceedings. Often, victims have complained that they had no idea a plea bargain had been reached or that a defendant had been sentenced. Similarly, victims wish to know when the prisoner convicted of a crime against them has been released, or has escaped, so that they can be as prepared as possible to encounter the offender. In response to these concerns, states have drafted legislation giving victims legal rights to a range of information about their cases. Increasingly, the case-specific rights to notice are implemented through an automated process whereby victims who have preregistered receive telephone calls from computerized notification systems.[39]

THE RIGHT TO BE PRESENT

Victims often want to see and hear the workings of the criminal justice process firsthand. Though many want to listen to how the crime is described in court, hear the arguments of the lawyers, and watch the reactions of the judge and jury, the process has often been closed to victims, who report that they have been excluded from critical proceedings, told to sit in the hallway as a trial proceeds, and were not allowed to hear a judge explain the sentence.

To address these concerns, most states now give victims a right to attend most criminal proceedings.[40] Even though these rights have limitations, they reflect a remarkable advance for crime victims, who are now entitled to watch the proceedings of their government as cases are prosecuted and adjudicated.

THE RIGHT TO BE HEARD

Many victims seek more than simply to be informed about the criminal justice system and allowed to observe proceedings. For example, many want to express their wishes before a prosecutor decides to negotiate a plea. Others feel that judges should understand the full impact of a crime before sentencing a defendant. Beginning in the 1970s, a number of victim advocates argued that victims should have a right to meaningful participation in the decisions being made about the crimes they experienced. A new legal role for victims emerged as they were granted the right to consultation before plea agreements, the right to provide victim impact statements, the right to be heard at sentencing, and the right to participate in parole hearings and in pardon or commutation proceedings.

Victim advocates' stunning political success means that today, thirty-two of the fifty states have amended their constitutions to include victims' rights, usually including the rights to be informed, present, and heard at critical stages of the process.[41] Every state has enacted statutes codifying many other victims' rights. Half the states give victims a general right to a speedy trial, or require that the court at least consider the victim's interests in ruling on a motion for continuance. Many states require prosecutors to consult with victims before making key decisions such as entering into plea agreements or declining to prosecute certain charges.[42]

It should be noted that in drafting victims' rights legislation, states define "victim" differently; some extend rights only to victims of violent crime, and others include victims of economic or property crime.[43] These disparities have created hierarchies of crime victims in which the victim of a street mugging who lost a small sum of money has the right to be notified, present, and heard during the criminal justice process, while the victim of a nonviolent identity theft who lost her life savings might not.

Despite much success from these efforts at a political level, criminal justice officials still treat crime victims in much the same way they did before the reforms. According to a study sponsored by the National Center for Victims of Crime that examined practices in states with strong legal rights for crime victims,[44] nearly two-thirds of victims were not informed of the pretrial release of the accused, half of all victims in cases resulting in plea agreements were not given an opportunity to consult with the prosecutor prior to the plea agreement, and nearly half were never notified of the sentencing hearing at all.[45]

These disappointing results have also been documented in a number of other studies.[46] It is common for victims not to know their rights.[47] Surveys of crime victims nationwide document that they are often not given information about their cases.[48] Most victims' rights are not implemented or enforced.[49] Victims are routinely denied their rights to be present and to participate at critical stages of criminal proceedings.[50]

In cases where restitution was an option, victims frequently complain that the judge did not consider restitution; others say it was not awarded, or if awarded, was not collected.[51] There is no national accounting of unpaid restitution, but experts estimate that the amount totals billions of dollars.[52] When unpaid fees, fines, and restitution are combined, the U.S. Department of Justice estimated that in 2002 about $25 billion went uncollected.[53] In 2007 the state of Pennsylvania estimated that $1.55 billion in fees, fines, and restitution remained unpaid.[54] At last count Arizona estimated $831 million in comparable unpaid monies.[55] Equally troubling, recent reports have highlighted the fact that even when restitution is collected, it is frequently not distributed. According to court officials, in the Los Angeles federal court district in 2005, roughly $4.7 million had not been distributed to more than 6,000 victims.[56]

This analysis leads to the disturbing conclusion that victims' rights are often empty promises, dependent for their implementation on the discretion of agencies of the justice system. In the words of prominent researchers Deborah Kelly and Edna Erez, "At base, victims' rights often remain privileges to be granted or denied depending on the whim of the police, the prosecutor, or the judge."[57]

Seen through a different lens, however, this disappointing outcome may not be surprising. As was documented in the previously discussed studies of the efforts to improve victim participation, criminal justice agencies are deeply resistant to meaningful participation by crime victims. This may reflect widespread discomfort with victims, but the reality is that the current criminal justice system was not designed to accommodate victims' needs, and the disincentives to consider their interests are strong.[58] Notwithstanding the significant progress in embedding new rights for victims in state and federal legislation, the core mission and culture of the justice system remains fundamentally unchanged.

The experience of victims throughout the criminal justice process would likely improve if states enacted enforcement mechanisms, created a culture of accountability, and remedied the shortfall between promise and reality. Meeting these objectives should be the next phase of the campaign to develop participatory rights for victims of crime. Absent such measures, we must face the reality that many victims will continue to feel ignored, excluded, and profoundly disrespected by criminal justice officials.

The Promise and Limits of Restorative Justice

Over the past two decades, reformers have been notably successful in promoting a new vision of justice, called "restorative justice." Its proponents advocate for alternatives to the traditional criminal justice process, which they characterize as overly retributive.[59] Rather than focusing on punishment as a response to crime, restorative justice emphasizes the interpersonal nature of crime, envisions a non-adversarial process, and seeks to repair the harm caused by criminal behavior. Howard Zehr, who has been called the father of restorative justice, defines it as "a process to involve, to the extent possible, those who have a stake in a specific offense and to collectively identify and address harms, needs, and obligations, in order to heal and put things as right as possible."[60]

Different models of restorative justice programs have emerged. Some involve encounters between victims and offenders, such as dialogues, conferences, or mediation and other forms of dispute resolution. Others reach beyond victims and offenders to include stakeholders from the community who might have been affected by the crime and have an interest in the outcome. Formats include family group conferences, sentencing circles, healing circles, and circles of support and accountability.[61]

From a victim's perspective, the concept of restorative justice holds great promise. Its embrace of healing as a central goal is appealing to many victims. Restorative justice programs envision a role for victims that can be more satisfying than their role in the traditional justice system, offering them an opportunity to tell their story. They may interact directly with the person who committed the crime, learning more about the incident and the underlying circumstances. They may experience empathy from the offender, in some cases leading to an apology or other expression of remorse. Other stakeholders such as the family of the offender, or a community leader, may express regret that the crime occurred and concern for the victim's well-being.

Compared to the more impersonal criminal justice process, which does not focus on the needs of victims, restorative justice programs present a wider range of positive options. Crime victims are more likely to receive restitution or reparation for harms. There is a greater opportunity to address underlying issues, resolve long-standing conflicts, and develop forward-looking relationships.

These restorative justice efforts, however, still fall short of providing a model justice process for crime victims.[62] A fundamental shortcoming of such programs is that they reach very few victims. Restorative justice initiatives typically operate within the context of the traditional criminal justice process, either as diversion programs in lieu of prosecution, or as post-sentencing mechanisms to promote healing and dialogue among offenders, victims, and affected members of the community. Because only a small percentage of victims are ever formally involved in much of the criminal justice process, either because the people who committed the crimes are never identified, or because even if known to the authorities, they are never arrested and prosecuted, most victims would never have the option of participating in a restorative justice program.

In addition, because most such programs require that the offender voluntarily agree to participate, and admit culpability before the process begins, the concept is further limited to those cases in which the offender meets both conditions. Finally, most restorative justice options are designed for categories of crimes; some are available only for minor crimes, or nonviolent crimes, others are only for cases approved by a prosecutor or judge. Thus the number of cases eligible for restorative justice becomes minute compared to the enormous number of crime victims in America.

Even for those few victims who are eligible, and who choose to participate in restorative justice programs, the results may be unsatisfying. Repairing the harm caused by crime is often complicated and may require far more than apologies, restitution, and relationship building. Reparation can require expert counseling, assistance with safety planning, relocation, and any number of services required to rebuild a life. It can require emergency daycare for the parent who needs to get a job to handle new crime-related expenses, substance abuse treatment for the traumatized victim who has turned to drugs, a companion for the victim now too afraid to leave home or go to the store alone, or employment counseling or training for victims who no longer can perform their old jobs. In many cases, government resources and services are required. If the resources available to repair the harms are limited to resources provided by the offender and community stakeholders involved in the restorative justice process, then many victims' needs will not be addressed.

This is not to say that offenders and communities should not be asked to help make victims whole again. On the contrary, their participation should be considered part of a just response to crime, and to the extent that restorative justice programs offer victims an opportunity to be heard, and a range of outcomes not available through the traditional criminal justice process, they represent important progress. Restorative justice, however, will probably always be available to, and appropriate for, small numbers of victims, and should thus be viewed as an optional component of a larger effort to provide victims the safety and justice they deserve.

Conclusion

This review of the evolution of our response to crime victims paints a mixed picture. On one hand, there has been substantial progress in creating a safety net for victims and conceptual breakthroughs in our jurisprudence that benefited hundreds of thousands of crime victims. In the span of a single generation we have witnessed the development of victim-centered services, the articulation of new roles for victims in criminal justice proceedings, overdue attention to the importance of supporting victims as they perform their civic duty in coming to court, and a serious movement to refashion our justice system in ways that address victims' needs.

But these reforms are incomplete. The shortfall of services compared to need is troubling. We have been unable to design a delivery system that routinely responds to the needs of all crime victims. Instead, we have created a highly fragmented system that provides better services to some categories of victims than to others, and employs distinctions such as that between victims of violent and nonviolent, or financial crime, that often bear little relationship to the harm experienced.[63]

At the same time, our reliance on the traditional criminal justice process as the primary way to provide justice for victims is flawed. Since most crimes are not prosecuted, a strategy to honor our obligations to victims that relies on rights to participate in criminal proceedings, or services delivered through a prosecutor's office, or even cases with identified offenders, is destined to fail to provide justice to most victims.

The philosophy of Parallel Justice starts with a different premise. All victims of crime, not just those whose offenders are prosecuted, are entitled to justice. All victims are entitled to safety and support as they rebuild their lives. Certainly, when victims participate in criminal proceedings, their voices should be heard, and their needs should be addressed as much as possible. They should be treated with compassion and respect, and they should be afforded all their legal rights. If the criminal justice process or alternative "restorative" programs offer some victims opportunities to learn more about the crime, secure restitution, hear an expression of remorse, or achieve a greater likelihood of safety, so much the better. But all victims of crime are entitled to a separate path to safety and justice, one that does not replace, but that runs parallel to, the criminal justice process.

3

The Parallel Justice Framework: Guiding Principles and Responsibilities

PARALLEL JUSTICE PROVIDES A NEW FRAMEWORK for responding to crime. Based on the premise that in addition to holding offenders accountable for the crimes they commit, society has a separate obligation to repair the harm experienced by victims, it fulfills the implicit promise made by our society when we define behavior as criminal. If society meets these obligations, then justice is served, because both the perpetrator and the victim of a crime receive fair and appropriate communal responses.

For every reported crime, our society would continue to respond by trying to apprehend, prosecute, sanction, and eventually reintegrate the offender back into productive communal life. Under a Parallel Justice framework, there would always be a separate set of responses for the individual who has been harmed by the crime. These responses would not depend on whether the person who committed the crime is ever identified or convicted in the criminal justice system. And, unlike restorative justice processes (described in chapter 2), Parallel Justice would not depend on the participation of an offender, or rely solely on the resources of individuals or organizations in a local community to meet a victim's needs. In all cases, the harm experienced by victims of crime would be acknowledged by our government, and addressed through a wide range of resources.

Parallel Justice decouples the pursuit of justice for victims from the administration of justice for offenders. As a result, justice for victims becomes a distinct goal rather than an occasional byproduct of a system focused elsewhere. By creating a separate path to justice for crime victims, one that responds to individual victims' experiences and channels assistance to victims from both the public and the private sectors, we elevate the goal of helping victims rebuild their lives to a fundamental component of society's pursuit of justice.

CHARTING THE COURSE OF PARALLEL JUSTICE RESPONSES

Within a Parallel Justice framework, society's obligation to a victim of crime would begin when that crime is committed. As soon as a crime is reported, in addition to all the traditional criminal justice responses seeking to identify the offenders and hold them accountable, government agencies and local communities would focus their efforts on keeping victims safe and decreasing the likelihood of repeat victimization. All victims would be offered immediate support, compensation for their losses, and practical assistance. When their more urgent needs have been met, they would be offered opportunities to describe the harms they have experienced and set forth what they need to get their lives back on track. Government officials would marshal as many resources as possible to meet their short- and long-term needs. In order to provide comprehensive and coordinated assistance, a wide range of government and community-based institutions would play an active role in helping victims of crime move on with their lives. These public and private resources would all be mobilized to ensure victims' continued safety, provide the support and counseling they need to overcome isolation and fear, and empower them to join productive community life. For all crimes — regardless of whether an offender is ever identified or convicted—our communal response to victims would include acknowledging the harms they have suffered, and doing everything we can to relieve them.

Parallel Justice is not an alternative to the criminal justice process, but rather an additional, often contemporaneous, set of responses geared to victims. Just as the criminal justice system seeks to be fair to offenders and create outcomes that are in the interest of society at large, this parallel set of responses should be designed to be fair to victims, and create outcomes that are in the best interest of society. Justice can be achieved through two separate paths with opportunities for interaction and connection between them.

Society's justice interests for victims and offenders are remarkably similar (see box 3.1). Safety is an important priority regarding both offenders and victims. We seek to keep offenders safe from vigilantism, and to protect communities from further harm they might inflict. At the same time, we must also keep the safety of victims a high priority and focus on preventing repeat victimization. Our communal response to offenders seeks accountability, with guarantees of due process during each phase of an investigation and prosecution. After a crime, irrespective of whether the person who committed the crime has been identified and prosecuted, our response to victims should be geared to keeping them safe and helping them recover from the trauma of the crime, while affording them all their legal rights.

A person accused of committing a crime is offered a forum, a day in court, which culminates in an adjudication and, if he or she is found guilty, a sentence imposed by a judge. If an alternative process such as a diversion program or mediation is used, there is also an outcome that reflects a communal response. Whether a sentence is designed to rehabilitate or punish, or an alternative process is primarily focused on helping the offender get back on track, society's ultimate goal, whenever possible, is reintegration of the offender into productive, law-abiding communal life. Similarly, victims should be provided a forum, an opportunity to describe the impact the crime has had on their lives, and seek a comprehensive response that provides the resources and services they need. Society's goal in structuring this comprehensive response should be reintegration of victims to healthy communal life. While full reintegration may not be possible for all victims, every effort should be made to reach that goal.

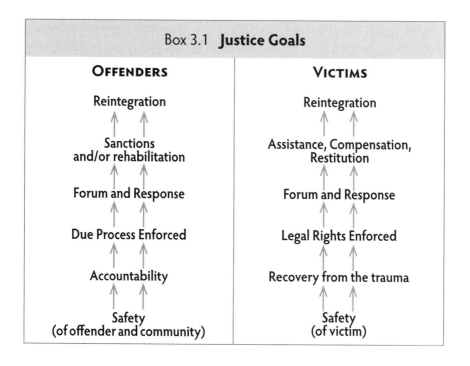

Box 3.1 **Justice Goals**	
OFFENDERS	**VICTIMS**
Reintegration	Reintegration
↑ ↑	↑ ↑
Sanctions and/or rehabilitation	Assistance, Compensation, Restitution
↑ ↑	↑ ↑
Forum and Response	Forum and Response
↑ ↑	↑ ↑
Due Process Enforced	Legal Rights Enforced
↑ ↑	↑ ↑
Accountability	Recovery from the trauma
↑ ↑	↑ ↑
Safety (of offender and community)	Safety (of victim)

GUIDING PRINCIPLES OF PARALLEL JUSTICE

As we construct this new response to victims of crime, we must recognize there is no blueprint to follow. Rather, the development of Parallel Justice initiatives will be guided by the ten principles below, which define a new framework for providing justice to victims of crime. In chapter 4, these principles are translated into a set of concrete examples of how Parallel Justice can be implemented "on the ground."

Justice Requires Helping Victims of Crime Rebuild Their Lives

A just society should respond to the needs of those who have been harmed by crime, in a way that is both fair and equitable to individual victims and good for society at large. Victims of crime need to feel safe again, to recover from the trauma of the crime, and to regain a sense of control over their lives. Individual victims and society at large both benefit when victims' needs are addressed through a communal response and victims are reintegrated into productive community life. Helping victims rebuild their lives is therefore an integral part of justice.

All Victims of Crime Deserve Justice

We need a universal approach that will provide justice to all victims of crime. Over the last three decades, as resources and services have been developed to assist crime victims, many have been offered only to certain categories of victims. It is a central tenet of Parallel Justice that justice, whether it is in the form of resources and assistance or the right to participate in the criminal justice system, should be provided to all victims, regardless of the nature of the crime. A hierarchy that designates some victims as more deserving than others is inconsistent with our basic concept of justice.

Our response to victims, and the services and resources we provide them, should be geared to their actual needs rather than stereotypes or assumptions about how different categories of victims experience crime. For example, all victims who want information about their case, want to confer with the prosecutor before a plea bargain, observe the criminal court process, or submit a victim impact statement should be encouraged and supported to do so. There is no principled reason to justify the creation of more participatory rights for victims of violent crime while denying those rights to victims of financial crime. Victims of any kind of crime should have the same legal rights to information about their cases, and to be present and participate during the criminal justice process.[1]

Finally, we must create communal responses that are set in motion at the occurrence of a crime, without waiting for the justice system to identify, prosecute, or convict a perpetrator of crime. It should not matter whether a victim initially reports a crime to a police officer, a healthcare official, or a victim advocate. It should not matter whether a crime was committed against a person on the street, in a prison, a mental institution, a nursing home, or a homeless shelter. It should not matter whether the offender is an individual or a corporation, or whether the crime is a mugging or a widespread corporate fraud. Our communal response should be triggered by the occurrence of a crime — any crime.

Victims of Crime Should Be Presumed Credible Unless There Is Reason to Believe Otherwise

One of the most common complaints voiced by victims is that in the aftermath of crime they feel alone and misunderstood. When they are disbelieved, or their experience is minimized by others, their alienation and distrust grows. It is particularly distressing to victims when someone to whom they have turned for assistance does not believe them, often reopening wounds inflicted by the initial act of intentional cruelty. We should avoid judgments about victims' credibility based purely on their affect, and recognize that victims react to crime in individualized and often unpredictable ways. We should presume that victims are credible, and respond to their needs, unless it becomes clear that they are not telling the truth.

Adherence to this principle will not only help individual victims, it will also promote community well-being. If victims are not believed, and are not provided the resources and assistance they deserve, it is more difficult for them to regain a sense of control over their lives, and ultimately our communities suffer as a result. For example, if victims are not believed by agents of the criminal justice system — often the first people victims turn to for help — the resulting alienation undercuts our ability to hold offenders accountable and to promote community safety. For both individual and societal reasons, we should assume that a person claiming to be a victim of crime is in fact a victim of crime, unless there is reason to believe otherwise.

Victim Safety Should Be a Top Priority

Perhaps the most fundamental goal of a just society is to provide for the safety of its citizens. Providing justice for crime victims often requires a heightened focus on safety. This is necessary for several reasons. First, the breach of the social contract that occurs when a crime is committed creates an additional obligation for society to shield victims from further harm. Second, given the research demonstrating increased vulnerability to repeat victimization following an initial incident, society should respond in a timely manner, taking steps to prevent further crime and violence. Finally, victims cannot move forward in their lives if they are unsafe or fearful. Therefore, every aspect of our communal response to victims must be designed to promote their safety.

Victims Should Experience No Further Harm

We should treat victims of crime with compassion, respect, and dignity. Individuals interacting with crime victims on a regular basis are particularly obliged to make every effort not to worsen the harms victims experience. The policies and practices of both government agencies and community-based institutions should reflect this principle. For example, we should remove barriers to services and resources, and make special allowances to expedite assistance for crime victims. Whenever possible, we should also eliminate crime-related administrative expenses and financial obligations now shouldered by victims.

Victims' Rights Should Be Implemented and Enforced

State and federal legislatures have created statutory and constitutional rights for victims of crime. These rights reflect a national recognition that crime victims are entitled to meaningful participation in the administration of justice. Yet little attention has been paid to implementing or enforcing these rights. We must ensure that victims' legal rights are implemented and that victims have access to effective enforcement mechanisms when they are not.

Victims Should Have Opportunities to Talk About Their Experience and Their Needs

Victims of crime need to be heard, and our society needs to listen. When victims articulate what they experienced and what they need, they regain a sense of control over their lives. Furthermore, as a society, we need to hear these personal accounts of crime to help us gain a deeper understanding of its impact, and ultimately to respond to victims more effectively. These opportunities for victims to talk about their experiences should exist within government and at the community level. In appropriate circumstances, victims should also be afforded opportunities to communicate with offenders, both to impart information about the impact of the crime and to learn more about the crime from the offender.

Victims Should Be Told that What Happened to Them Was Wrong and that Every Effort Will Be Made to Help Them Rebuild Their Lives

Our communal response to victims must be just as explicit as our response to offenders. It is essential that victims are told that what happened to them was wrong. At the same time, they should know that action will be taken to help them. This acknowledgment of harm is simple, and yet, along with a demonstration of support, it can be extremely important to victims.

Victim's Needs Should Be Addressed Through a Coordinated, Comprehensive Communal Response

Once victims have described what happened to them, and have stated what they need to move on with their lives, justice requires that we respond. For every victim who seeks help, we should provide individualized, comprehensive, and coordinated assistance that addresses the needs victims have defined.

Victims' responses to crime can involve many stages, from the initial crisis reactions through long-term efforts to put the experience behind them. Emergency assistance, compensation to ease the burden of their losses, and services and resources to address particular crime-related challenges, may all be necessary at different points along the way. Gearing our response to victims' specific needs, and offering all the immediate and ongoing assistance we can afford, will go a long way toward helping them recover from the harms sustained as a result of crime.

Decisions About How to Address Victims' Needs Should Be Based On Sound Information and Research

Responding to victims' needs effectively requires an accurate understanding of the impact of crime in local communities and solid research evaluating the effectiveness of different interventions and programs. Communities can employ a variety of methods—including talking directly to victims—to gather information about the incidence and prevalence of crime, and the harms experienced by individuals and communities.

Box 3.2 GUIDING PRINCIPLES OF PARALLEL JUSTICE

- ▶ Justice requires helping victims of crime rebuild their lives.
- ▶ All victims of crime deserve justice.
- ▶ All victims should be presumed credible unless there is reason to believe otherwise.
- ▶ Victims' safety should be a top priority.
- ▶ Victims should experience no further harm.
- ▶ Victims' rights should be implemented and enforced.
- ▶ Victims should have opportunities to talk about their experience and their needs.
- ▶ Victims should be told what happened to them was wrong, and that every effort will be made to help them rebuild their lives.
- ▶ Victims' needs should be addressed through a comprehensive, coordinated communal response.
- ▶ Decisions about how to address victims' needs should be based on sound information and research.

WHO IS RESPONSIBLE FOR PROVIDING JUSTICE TO VICTIMS?

In order to translate these principles of Parallel Justice into an operational reality, it is important to understand the distinct roles that must be played by each of the components of the "communal response" that constitutes justice for victims of crime. Government must play a critical role in implementing Parallel Justice. This governmental role is a logical corollary to the designation of certain misconduct as a crime: government has an obligation not only to apprehend and prosecute those who break the law, but also to repair the harm done to victims. But this is not solely a governmental obligation. Communities and offenders should also foster Parallel Justice, and their actions, like the government's, should be guided by the principles of Parallel Justice outlined above.

THE ROLE OF GOVERNMENT IN PARALLEL JUSTICE

Parallel Justice envisions an integral and central role for society at large, represented by the government, in repairing the harm caused by crime, and extending to every victim of crime. No matter whether the crime is violent or nonviolent, and whether the offender is apprehended and tried or not, all victims are entitled to a comprehensive societal response, with their government taking the lead. While different agencies and even different branches of government may assume a more prominent role in implementing various aspects of Parallel Justice, we must recognize obligations to victims of crime that extend throughout government at the local, state, and federal levels. The many levels and agencies of government should work together to provide justice to victims. Our government should:

Foster Commitment to Help Victims
Of Crime Rebuild Their Lives

The foundation of Parallel Justice is the public will to help victims of crime rebuild their lives. The government must foster this commitment by developing policies, services, and resources to promote the reintegration of all victims. Government-sponsored research and publications on victim-related issues, conferences and hearings on the impact of crime, and programmatic initiatives that address victims' needs are also necessary. Government officials should actively encourage public discourse about how the powerful and often life-changing impact of crime ultimately produces negative consequences for all of society. Legislatures should monitor the executive and judicial branches of government to make sure they are implementing policies and procedures that promote Parallel Justice.

Ensure that the Goal of Victim Safety Is
Reflected In All Policies and Practices

Every government agency should examine its operations to determine the most effective ways to maximize the safety of crime victims and prevent repeat victimization. Victim safety must be an important factor in decision-making during every stage of the criminal justice process, from the initial interview with victims, to setting bail conditions and plea agreements, through sentencing, corrections, and parole. This requires communication with victims at each stage of the process. In many cases interventions must begin as soon as possible to prevent repeat victimization. Moreover, many victims participating in the criminal justice process are subjected to new threats and other forms of harassment, so we must make every effort to keep them safe before, during, and after a trial.

Similarly, the protocols of social service and healthcare agencies administered or regulated by government must emphasize the importance of keeping victims safe. From intake and record-keeping procedures through counseling, training, or medical treatment, procedures must maximize victims' safety and prevent their re-victimization.

Provide Emergency, Transitional, and Ongoing Assistance as Needed

While neighbors, families, and local communities can all provide critical assistance to victims, it is the responsibility of government to ensure that victims are offered a comprehensive continuum of care. All victims should be attended to soon after a crime occurs. All should be offered a variety of services, including supportive counseling and psychotherapy, safety planning, and practical assistance such as new locks for smashed doors and new glass for broken windows. After the initial crisis, services must continue to meet victims' ongoing needs. Working with the public and private sectors, the government should marshal resources needed to address victims' long-term, often complicated problems such as transportation, daycare, employment counseling and training, substance abuse treatment, and housing.

Offer Priority Access to Resources and Services

Many crime-related needs of victims can be met through the assistance of social service providers outside the traditional victim services networks. For instance, a woman who has been mugged and is afraid to leave her home might benefit from special transportation services perhaps originally created for the elderly. A victim of sexual assault or child abuse who uses drugs to numb the pain could benefit from drug treatment. A victim of a bank robbery may be too traumatized to return to her job at the bank, and could benefit from employment counseling and training to find a new job. Whenever possible, to honor our obligations to victims of crime, government at all levels should give victims priority access to resources and services that would address crime-related needs.

Provide Victims Compensation for Crime-related Expenses

Victim compensation serves as both an explicit governmental recognition that what happened to a victim was wrong, and a tangible expression of communal support. As discussed in chapter 2, all victims of crime should be eligible for compensation. In addition to reimbursement for economic losses such as immediate out-of-pocket expenses associated with the crime, compensation should also include coverage for ongoing crime-related expenses including employment training, counseling, transportation, and healthcare. Finally, a just compensation program would include payments for pain and suffering as well.

Create Special Allowances to Ease Victims' Burdens

In the aftermath of September 11, the federal government and several states passed creative legislation and developed innovative policies to ease the burdens facing the victims of the attacks. This remarkable response to a national tragedy demonstrates the importance of governmental leadership in helping victims respond to the impact of crime. Our challenge is to learn from this experience and adapt these policy reforms—and others like them—to benefit victims of everyday crimes. For example, all levels of government should provide tax relief, low-interest loans, and significant flexibility regarding other legal obligations that can be difficult for victims to meet in the aftermath of crime.

Implement and Enforce Victims' Rights

As a nation, we have created an expectation that defendants' due process rights will be upheld, not only because it is good for individual offenders, but also because these rights reflect our values and our aspirations as to how our society should treat all of its citizens. Justice requires that we develop a similar expectation that victims' rights will be upheld because they reflect the proper relationship between our society and its citizens. Accordingly, every agency of government must implement and enforce relevant victims' rights. All government officials must understand that protecting victims' rights is their responsibility. Every level of government must develop mechanisms to ensure that these rights are enforced. If rights are created but not honored or enforced, they become meaningless.

Ensure Fair and Respectful Treatment of Victims

Every victim should be treated with compassion, respect, and decency. The element of intentional cruelty inherent in most crimes leaves victims with a sense of alienation and isolation, and sometimes a fear of others. The actions of government officials are particularly important to victims because these officials represent society at large. Poor treatment of victims exacerbates alienation and distrust. Compassion helps victims overcome the trauma they have experienced and reconnect with their community.

Provide Opportunities for Victims to Talk About Their Experience and Their Needs

The government has the authority and the obligation to marshal resources to address the complicated and long-term problems many victims experience. To maximize the effectiveness of these efforts, governments should offer victims two different kinds of opportunities to describe the full impact of the harms they have suffered and the services and support they need to move forward.

First, throughout government, and particularly within the criminal justice process, every agency should have mechanisms in place to facilitate regular and ongoing communication with victims. To make informed decisions victims need information, and they need to know their options. In essence, victims of crime should be viewed as consumers of government services who merit special attention.

Second, every jurisdiction should also offer a separate forum where victims, if they choose to, can explain the full impact of the crime they have experienced. This forum is a new government entity created to implement an important process in Parallel Justice. As discussed below, these forums allow officials an opportunity to acknowledge that what happened to victims was wrong, and to coordinate resources and services on their behalf. In addition, the information gathered at these forums should enable governments to address gaps in services, and change policies or practices that are contrary to the principles of Parallel Justice. Finally, victims themselves need to be heard. It is beneficial to know that someone, particularly their government, cares enough to take the time to listen.

Acknowledge That What Happened to Victims Was Wrong and That Every Effort Will Be Made to Help Them Rebuild Their Lives

Just as only the government can marshal the range of resources victims need, only the government can speak on behalf of society at large and provide a communal response to victims acknowledging that what happened to them was wrong. Specific statements to this effect can be incorporated into many of the written and oral communications between government officials and victims. This is a powerful message coming from the government, and particularly meaningful when it includes a strong commitment of ongoing support.

Develop and Coordinate a Comprehensive Communal Response to Victims

To address victims' needs effectively, the government should draw upon and coordinate a broad spectrum of resources in both the private and public sectors, including traditional victim services, as well as a range of other options to help them get their lives back on track. Steps should be taken to ensure that historically under-served populations of victims are reached.

Base Decisions About How to Address Victims' Needs on Sound Information and Research

In order to develop the most useful resources for victims, jurisdictions need up-to-date, accurate information about victims' experiences of crime and its impact on their lives. Government, at all levels, should invest in a knowledge base of information and research on victims of crime that guides our communal response. For example, decisions about how to address victims' needs should be informed by regular household victimization surveys and interviews with victims. These can provide objective, efficient, and useful ways to assess the needs of victims in a particular state or community, and track progress in meeting those needs. Government should also provide sufficient funding to evaluate government-funded responses to victims, and encourage efforts to improve victim services based on the latest research findings.

Box 3.3 THE ROLE OF GOVERNMENT

- ▶ Foster commitment to help victims of crime rebuild their lives.
- ▶ Ensure that the goal of victim safety is reflected in all policies and practices.
- ▶ Provide victims emergency and ongoing assistance as needed.
- ▶ Offer victims priority access to resources and services.
- ▶ Provide compensation to victims for crime-related expenses.
- ▶ Create special allowances to ease victims' burdens.
- ▶ Implement and enforce victims' rights.
- ▶ Ensure fair and respectful treatment of victims.
- ▶ Provide opportunities for victims to talk about their experience and their needs.
- ▶ Acknowledge that what happened to victims was wrong and that every effort will be made to help them rebuild their lives.
- ▶ Develop and coordinate a comprehensive, communal response to victims.
- ▶ Base decisions about how to address victims' needs on sound information and research.

THE ROLE OF COMMUNITIES

Communities can play a vital role in providing a just response to victims of crime, and should be encouraged to participate in a number of ways. Just as society at large, acting through our government, communicates important principles of justice, so too the actions of neighbors and community-based institutions should reinforce the basic principles of Parallel Justice. At the local neighborhood level, our communal response to victims can be particularly personal and can help reweave the fabric of community life. With this in mind, local communities should:

Foster Commitment to Help
Victims of Crime Rebuild Their Lives

In many ways, American communities have already embraced the idea of reaching out to neighbors in need. Schools, faith-based organizations, and neighborhood associations have long supported our national tradition of providing emotional support to neighbors who are sick, bereaved, or experiencing other hardships.

Crime victims often report that the most valuable support they received was from neighbors and family members. What is lacking, however, is community-level commitment to provide this kind of assistance consistently. Just as government leaders should promote the public will to provide justice to victims of crime, local community leaders and civic institutions can foster the notion that all members of a community, and all community institutions, have an obligation to participate in these efforts. Given the enormous social value of reintegrating victims into community life as soon as possible, community institutions should work together to nurture a deeper commitment to victims, and explicitly emphasize the value of providing assistance.

Embrace the Obligation to Keep Victims Safe

In a just society, safety is everyone's responsibility. Embracing this obligation requires residents, local businesses, and community-based organizations to make every effort to promote safety generally, and especially to keep individual victims of crime safe from further harm. Victims should be able to seek assistance from their neighbors and communities in managing safety plans, rely on local shops and businesses to provide safe haven, and count on other community members to report activity that might lead to repeat victimization. Activating these resources on behalf of crime victims requires articulating a community-level commitment to ensure their safety.

Listen to Victims with Compassion

In addition to talking to government officials about the crime and its impact, it can be helpful for victims to share their experiences with members of their community. These interactions can occur in public settings including faith institutions, tenant organizations, parent-teacher associations, or in the privacy of neighbors' homes. They can also occur in community-sponsored restorative justice programs. A just community should provide many opportunities for victims to talk about the aftermath of crime, and to express their needs. While many victims will have no desire to engage in these discussions, and should not be pressured to do so, all victims should know that if they do wish to talk, someone will take the time to listen with compassion and without judgment.

Provide Support to Victims Through Resources and Practical Assistance

Victims of crime typically have a variety of needs. Some require professional attention such as psychotherapy or legal services, but many others can be addressed by neighbors and family members. Whether it is through offers of child-care, prepared meals, or just looking in on a homebound victim, neighbors can provide critical assistance unlikely to come from other sources. Communities can also mobilize local businesses, civic associations, and other community-based organizations to provide support and resources congruent with their daily operations, yet tailored to meet the specific needs of victims in their communities. The human kindness evident in community level support relieves many of the burdens crime victims face, mitigates the cruelty of crime, and helps victims regain their trust and confidence in other people.

> BOX 3.4 **THE ROLE OF COMMUNITIES**

- ► Foster commitment to help victims of crime rebuild their lives.
- ► Embrace the obligation to keep victims safe.
- ► Listen to victims with compassion.
- ► Provide support to victims through resources and practical assistance.

THE ROLE OF OFFENDERS

People who commit crime can have an important role in providing justice to victims, but contact between victims and offenders can also be problematic. For example, offenders can help keep victims safe, or their actions can result in repeat victimization. Similarly, offenders can help victims move on with their lives in powerful ways, but they can also cause additional hardship. Because of these risks, offenders' interactions with victims should be monitored and in some cases carefully prescribed. Furthermore, certain positive behaviors should be encouraged, both by government officials and community members. In a Parallel Justice framework, people who commit crime should:

Acknowledge Responsibility for Their Actions

At the most fundamental level, offenders can contribute to victims' well-being in ways nobody else can by acknowledging that they committed the crime. Statements by offenders, taking responsibility for their actions, have tremendous value for victims, and are often greatly appreciated even in the absence of any other communication or action. While some offenders can also offer victims information about the circumstances of the crime, demonstrate remorse, or offer an apology, a simple acknowledgment of responsibility, in and of itself, is a powerful statement affirming a victim's experience.

When appropriate, offenders should also be encouraged to acknowledge the impact of their crimes on victims, and to do all that they can to repair the harms they have caused. Interactions between victims and offenders can be facilitated in a number of ways, including through corrections, probation, and parole departments, mediation and restorative justice programs, or other community-based organizations.

Do No Further Harm

In a just society that promotes the safety of victims and helps them regain control of their lives, every effort should be made to prevent repeat victimization of any kind, and to ensure that people who commit crime do no further harm. Offenders should not be allowed to harass or threaten victims in any way. If court orders of protection are in place, they should be enforced. As a general rule, people who commit crime should be expected to follow victims' requests regarding limitations on contact and other forms of communication.

Pay Restitution

Restitution typically consists of payment or benefits provided by an offender to a victim to reimburse the victim for crime-related losses. Just as compensation from the government demonstrates a communal obligation to victims, restitution confirms a separate obligation owed by offenders to victims to help repair the harms they have caused. In all cases where victims have experienced losses, the people who have committed the crimes should be ordered to pay restitution consistent with their ability to pay, and those orders should be enforced.

Box 3.5 THE ROLE OF OFFENDERS

- ▸ Acknowledge responsibility for their actions.
- ▸ Do no further harm.
- ▸ Pay restitution.

CONCLUSION

Parallel Justice represents a new way of thinking about how society can respond to victims of crime. If we follow the Parallel Justice principles, and encourage the active participation of offenders, communities and governments in Parallel Justice initiatives, we will change our justice paradigm. Instead of asking victims to seek justice solely through the criminal justice process, we would ask victims to define the problems they face, and then do our best to address them. Our goal would be to provide justice to victims by helping them rebuild their lives.

Consistent with Parallel Justice principles, we would offer emergency assistance to any crime victim who needed it, just as the Red Cross seeks to do for victims of hurricanes, floods, and now terrorism. Neighbors, religious institutions, civic groups, and block associations would be mobilized to offer support and comfort to all crime victims in their communities—homicide survivors, and victims of assault, rape, identity theft, burglary, or car crashes caused by drunk drivers—just as they often support people in their community who are sick or elderly.

Government officials following these principles would feel it is their responsibility to restore victims' safety and to decrease the likelihood of repeat victimization. All victims who fear for their safety would be offered emergency housing and assistance. In addition to sheltering battered women, we would seek to protect victims of gang violence, sexual assault, elder abuse, or burglary—essentially any intimidated victims or witnesses who can no longer live in their homes or neighborhoods without fear. All victims of crime, not just of violent crime, would have legal rights to respectful treatment and meaningful participation in the criminal justice system, and those rights would be enforced.

Using the Parallel Justice framework, communities throughout the country would provide victims opportunities to describe what happened to them and what they need to get their lives back on track.

Helping crime victims would be a government priority, ensuring sufficient resources and services for victims to move forward. We would respond to every victim of any kind of crime with the same level of creativity and commitment we brought to victims of the September 11 attacks. By engaging both the public and private sectors, and creating the public will to help victims of crime rebuild their lives, we would create a society in which justice required no less.

Our nation's concept of justice for victims must become part of our shared American values. Every schoolchild in America knows the *Miranda* warnings and the values they reflect. They know that if they are ever accused of violating the law, they will have certain due process rights—to remain silent, to have an attorney, to be presumed innocent until proven guilty. In the future, all children should also know that, if they ever become victims of crime, they have a right to be heard and a right to fair and respectful treatment. They should know that if they become victims of crime, their community and their government will help them rebuild their lives. Every child should understand that our American values include a commitment to Parallel Justice.

4

Creating Parallel Justice
On the Ground

THE PRINCIPLES OF PARALLEL JUSTICE and the roles envisioned for governments, communities, and offenders set forth in chapter 3 can guide significant transformation of the way society interacts with victims of crime. Chapter 4 paints a picture of how Parallel Justice can be implemented. The examples of "on the ground" initiatives that follow are not an exhaustive list of all the ways agencies and organizations could change their operations, but rather provide a sampling of realistic options for how to realign policies and practices to promote Parallel Justice.

This chapter begins with a discussion of ways to reorient the functions of criminal justice agencies. These agencies are particularly critical to the successful implementation of Parallel Justice because they have significant contact with victims of crime, represent the authority of government, and have great capacity to help or harm victims in important ways. The chapter continues with examples of initiatives in the healthcare and social service systems that are consistent with the principles of Parallel Justice, and then discusses ways employers, businesses, neighbors, friends, and family members can join the communal response to victims. Next, it discusses how the Parallel Justice framework creates opportunities for victim advocates and service providers to extend their reach. It goes on to describe legislative initiatives to provide more financial assistance to victims and mechanisms to enforce victims' rights. The chapter concludes with a discussion of victim compensation, and forums where victims can describe what happened to them and seek assistance.

THE POLICE

When considering what Parallel Justice looks like "on the ground," police departments have an enormous amount to contribute to the effort. For most victims, the first government official they encounter after the crime is an employee of the local police department. It may be the 911 operator who takes the victim's call, or the police officer who responds to the scene of the crime. It may be a detective who comes to a victim's home to take a statement, examine evidence, or assess the credibility of witnesses. In certain cases, a victim may interact with a special police unit established to respond to victims of sexual assault, domestic violence, child abuse, or hate crimes. If property has been seized as evidence, interactions with the police department may include the police employees who maintain the auto pound or the property clerk's office.

When the police respond to a crime, the victim may be disoriented, upset, and in many cases, traumatized. Police must ascertain whether a crime has been committed, gather evidence, and determine the identity of the offender. For a number of reasons, they may show little concern for the mental, emotional, or physical state of the victim. They may be pressed for time, they may not understand what the victim is going through, or they may think it is not their job to prevent further harm from occurring to a victim.

The Parallel Justice principles lead to an expanded role for the police, characterized by five specific commitments, described in detail below—to presume victims are credible, keep victims safe, inform victims of their rights, partner with victims in problem-solving, and treat victims with respect and sensitivity. These commitments operationalize principles of Parallel Justice.

Presume That Victims Are Credible

When police officers respond to a call, one of their first priorities is to interview victims and witnesses and determine whether, assuming that everything alleged is true, a crime was committed. In other words, the police must ascertain whether the facts as asserted meet the legal criteria of a violation of criminal law. The police also determine what crime—precisely which section of the penal law—the events would constitute if they prove to be true. These critical, preliminary determinations of the nature of the events are made every time police respond to a call.

In most jurisdictions, police will write a "complaint report" that indicates the victim's account of the event, and whether the complaint was unfounded or should be investigated. The report thus serves to either halt or set in motion continued criminal justice involvement. Consistent with Parallel Justice, a complaint should not be labeled unfounded unless the complainant is not credible, or if the events as described would not constitute a crime.

The complaint report should also be used to trigger Parallel Justice responses, but should not be required for victims to access needed services. For example, while most states ask people applying for victim compensation to attach a copy of a police complaint form to their application to demonstrate that they reported the crime, the federal guidelines for state victim compensation programs under the Victims of Crime Act (VOCA), do not require victims to have filed a police report. A victim's safety concerns, health, age, psychological condition, and any cultural or linguistic barriers can be considered legitimate reasons for the absence of a police report.[1] Most jurisdictions explicitly allow the recommendation of a victim advocate or health care official to substitute for a police report so the victim can qualify for compensation. Although Parallel Justice initiatives are likely to promote victim participation in the criminal justice process, exceptions such as these allow victims who have not reported their crimes to the police to access Parallel Justice responses.

Moreover, when a police officer does not believe someone who claims to be a victim of a crime, that person should be able to "appeal" that determination to a supervisor or other high-ranking police official. Laws should be enacted requiring police departments to make annual reports to legislative oversight committees documenting how many victims appealed the initial determinations by police officers, and the results of those appeals. This appeal process and the oversight procedures serve two purposes: they counteract the incentives police organizations experience to record fewer incidents of crime in order to keep rates of reported crime low, and they send a clear message to the public that the police response to victims matters, and that it is carefully monitored.

Keep Victims Safe

Given the high risk of repeat victimization, the principles of Parallel Justice require police to place a high priority on their obligation to keep victims safe. Because the time between the initial crime and a subsequent crime varies by crime category and by location,[2] police departments should regularly analyze local crime data to identify patterns of repeat victimization.

Documenting repeat victimization requires recordkeeping specifically designed to create victimization histories and track police responses and outcomes.[3] Community-wide analysis of repeat victimization involves several tasks, including mapping crime locations, sorting offenses by addresses and by victim names, counting both individual victims and specific offenses, and calculating the patterns of criminal activity.[4] While crime reports are most frequently used to document repeat victimization, police can gather additional information in the initial interview with a victim by asking about previous incidents, and making it a priority to survey victims after an investigation has been completed to determine whether subsequent, unreported crimes have occurred.

Police departments committed to keeping victims safe will emphasize the importance of the first contact between victims and officers. Police should determine, with victims, how they can be safe immediately and what steps they can take to be safe in the future. Victims who are regularly threatened (e.g., victims of domestic violence, sexual assault, or stalking, and elder abuse victims who are intimidated by relatives and fear remaining at home) should be advised about the availability of emergency housing. A victim who has been assaulted or harassed by someone with whom they have ongoing contact should be advised about orders of protection. A victim of burglary whose windows have been broken can be assisted in getting them repaired. A victim who was mugged on a dark street near her home can be assisted in working with neighbors and government agencies to create better lighting.

Preventing repeat victimization, however, is an ongoing obligation. Effective safety planning requires exploration of all the ways a victim may be vulnerable. Reasons for this vulnerability may include victims' habits, their location, their relative isolation, and the security level of their homes. Offenders may also have learned other relevant information during the commission of the crime, such as where keys are kept, what valuable items are in the house, or whether someone has a guard dog. This may determine whether another crime will be planned. The police should gather such information to assess the likelihood of repeat victimization and to design individual safety plans with victims.

Victim advocates can bring a useful perspective to safety planning. The woman who is considering relocating to escape a stalker, or the adult child who wants to involve family members in confronting someone who has abused an elderly parent, or the worker who continues at a job where there has been violence, would all benefit from the services of an advocacy organization. A victim advocate is often better suited to explore the emotional, social, financial, and legal aspects of the decisions.

Partnering with victim service providers, police can also provide concrete resources to keep victims safe. For example, in New York

City, Safe Horizon, the nation's largest victim services agency, receives funding from the city government to operate Project Safe, which will change the lock on a crime victim's door free of charge within the first twenty-four hours after the request is made. Police have been referring crime victims to Project Safe since 1979, when it first began.

Police can also work with victims to activate other resources in their community to help keep them safe. For instance, police should explore with victims the possibility of creating a "cocoon," a concept first developed in England.[5] With the victim's permission, a cocoon enlists family members, neighbors, and others who are given specific information regarding the safety risks faced by a particular victim, and are encouraged to call the police whenever they believe the victim is at risk.

For example, when a single mother has an order of protection against a stalker, family members, neighbors, and coworkers could be given a photograph of the stalker, as well as the information that the stalker is not supposed to be within a certain distance of the victim's home or workplace, a playground, or anywhere else she and her child go on a regular basis. They could be asked to call the police if they see that person at any off-limits location. So even if the victim doesn't observe the violation herself, there is a greater likelihood that it will be reported and can be addressed quickly to prevent additional violations.

A second example: If a victim in an apartment complex is at risk of domestic violence, a cocoon might be created with neighbors told that a certain signal—say, two knocks on the floor, or a light in a designated window—indicates that the victim is in danger. Recognizing the signal, neighbors would immediately know to call the police.

A final example: if a victim's house has been burglarized, both the police and the victim might want to share this information with neighbors to create a heightened alert, to encourage them to watch the victim's premises more carefully and report certain kinds of behavior quickly.

Unlike the more traditional neighborhood watch programs in

which neighbors are asked to be the "eyes and ears of the police" and report any suspicious activity, in a cocoon, neighbors are asked to take action when they observe specific activities that pose a risk to a particular victim—activity that might otherwise appear to be entirely lawful. Cocoons activate the under-utilized resource of family and neighborhood networks to partner with police to enhance the safety of victims of crime.

Finally, police departments are typically very effective at allocating resources based on organizational priorities. Information about repeat victimization can help police determine the most appropriate level of response and the most effective interventions following a particular incident. New protocols informed by an assessment of an individual victim's vulnerabilities can define the graduated responses that specify the type and degree of intervention according to the risk of revictimization.[6] In this way, the police officers responding to a crime report will provide assistance to a victim that is guided by a policy protocol, informed by research, and tailored to the victim's unique circumstances.

Inform Victims of Their Rights

Most states require police to inform victims about local victim services, victim compensation, and victims' rights in the criminal justice system. For most victims, this is the only way they will get this information. Most victims, however, do not receive this critical information, even in those jurisdictions where police are mandated by law to provide it.[7] Consistent with Parallel Justice principles, the police should be held accountable for providing this information to victims.

Police also have an obligation to make sure that crime victims are informed about the criminal investigation process, including what is likely to happen next in their case, whether there will be an investigation and by whom, the likelihood of an arrest, and when they will next be contacted by the police. If the police have seized property as evidence, victims should be told how to claim that property.

Police officers are accustomed to informing people they arrest about their legal rights pursuant to the Supreme Court's *Miranda* decision. Following Parallel Justice principles, the police would have a parallel obligation to inform victims of their legal rights. The police should explain these rights to victims, and distribute information cards describing them. Victims have important participatory rights—the right to be notified about important stages in the criminal justice process, to be conferred with before a plea is entered, to attend court proceedings, and to enter a victim impact statement at the time of sentencing—but they can only take advantage of these opportunities if they know about them.

Finally, the police can serve as a gateway to resources and services that are necessary to helping victims rebuild their lives—compensation, healthcare, social services, emergency housing, mental health counseling, all services that victims can either access directly or with the assistance of a victim advocate. Police should describe the kinds of assistance local victim services can provide, and set forth in general terms the extent of coverage under victim compensation. It is much more helpful to victims to hear a description of the available services than just to receive a phone number.

Because crime is often a very isolating experience, police should play an important role in connecting victims to the help they need. The role envisioned for police under Parallel Justice is not that they deliver these social services themselves, but rather that they make informative and useful referrals.

Partner with Victims on Problem-solving

Victims are key stakeholders not only in the investigation of crime but also in efforts to prevent a recurrence. Though they often have important information to contribute, victims are frequently overlooked as resources in problem-solving and prevention efforts. In the immediate, sometimes emotional, aftermath of crime, victims may provide little information and may not know what information would be useful to police. If police work with victims as partners throughout the course of an investigation, victims are likely to be more forthcoming, and as a result, police will solve and prevent more crimes. These partnerships, which encourage the active involvement of victims, have the added benefit of helping victims regain a sense of control over their lives.

Treat Victims with Respect and Sensitivity

In many respects, the police represent not only the criminal justice system but also the face of society at large. Victims frequently report that long after the crime occurred, it is the manner of the responding police officer that remains foremost in their minds. An officer who demonstrates compassion when responding to a call, or during especially difficult moments such as a death notification, or when a new lead has arisen in a cold case, can make a world of difference in a victim's experience.

If, in the aftermath of crime, victims feel that the police blame them for the crime, disbelieve them, or trivialize their experience, they are less likely to share the information with anyone else or seek additional help. By contrast, when police demonstrate concern, tell victims explicitly that what happened to them was wrong, and actively engage them in problem-solving and safety planning, victims are more likely to remain hopeful, feel they are regaining control over their lives, and have confidence in the authority of government and the criminal justice process.

For example, the Police Department of Redlands, California, under the leadership of Chief Jim Bueermann, has incorporated the principles of Parallel Justice into its vision for community policing. One of the department's five guiding principles is to "help victims of crime rebuild their lives." Consistent with this mission, the Redlands Police Department created a special Web site for victims to talk to each other about their experiences and share strategies to regain control of their lives. While the department prescreens the viewers and participants, victims are able to discuss the impact crime has had on them, seek help, and provide it to others. In addition to helping victims feel less isolated and powerless, the department uses the Web site to communicate crime prevention strategies and encourage victims to take advantage of available services. Each member of the department, uniformed and civilian alike, at all levels, has been encouraged to pursue Parallel Justice, with creative results. Early in the initiative, 911 operators in Redlands decided to send crime victims cards saying, "You are in our thoughts" thirty days after the initial call.

Another way the police can treat victims with respect and sensitivity is to make sure their policies and procedures do not impose unnecessary additional burdens on victims. For instance, many police departments impose fees for copies of complaint reports and storage of stolen vehicles, and leave victims liable for the cost of home repairs due to damage caused by searches. Parallel Justice would require the police to absorb these expenses rather than create more financial burdens or hardship for victims. For example, Utah passed legislation that waives or refunds the fee charged for the impoundment of a vehicle if the registered owner, lien holder, or owner's agent presents written evidence that the vehicle was stolen at the time it was impounded.[8]

Police should also provide emergency funds for victims in crisis who do not have adequate resources to cover additional expenses caused by the crime. For example, whenever necessary, the police should disburse small amounts of money to repair locks or broken windows, and provide taxi fare to a relative's house following a break-in or an assault. Police departments should be able to make arrangements to be reimbursed by the state victim compensation board for such emergency service expenses.

Finally, just as jurisdictions measure response time (the time it takes to respond to 911 calls) to assess the effectiveness of police services, police should also be held accountable for the quality of their interactions with crime victims. Questions designed to measure victims' assessments of police services could be incorporated into local household victimization surveys, or become part of separate consumer feedback initiatives conducted by police or local governments.

In 2001, the Metropolitan Police Department in Washington, D.C., conducted telephone interviews with randomly selected victims of crime to determine their level of satisfaction with police response.

The police received good grades for officer interaction skills. Most victims felt the officers were respectful, showed concern, listened without judging, and made them feel at ease. The survey also demonstrated that the department could improve its response by consistently providing appropriate referrals to services and crime prevention assistance, informing victims of their rights, and providing information about crime-victim compensation.[9]

As the preceding discussion illustrates, the Parallel Justice framework creates a different relationship between the police and crime victims. Parallel Justice requires police to treat victims with compassion and respect, make special allowances when appropriate, embrace their obligation to keep victims safe and prevent repeat victimization, provide information about the criminal justice system, and refer victims to social service providers and victim advocates to help them rebuild their lives. Though relatively simple, this shift in police priorities represents a fundamentally different societal response to crime victims.

THE PROSECUTOR

In the American criminal justice system, the prosecutor is the community's highest-ranking elected law enforcement official. As such, the prosecutor's role is to litigate criminal cases on behalf of the State, or the People. The prosecutor represents society at large, and does not represent individual victims in the sense in which lawyers typically represent individual clients.

The prosecutor's role is often misunderstood by victims, who expect prosecutors to be their lawyers, to consult with them before important decisions are made, and to represent their interests. The harsh reality of the process — from initial determination of charges to the actual trial — is that the victim is not represented by anyone.

Seen against the backdrop of a victim's overall experience, learning that they are essentially unrepresented in criminal trials can add to a sense of alienation and isolation. When victims are asked to testify, they are often disappointed if they are excluded from the courtroom beforehand, and later perplexed to learn that they are not allowed to talk about the impact of the crime during the trial phase. After sentencing proceedings, if they did provide a victim impact statement, they can be confused or angry when their views did not seem to influence the disposition of the case.

Prosecutors must make every effort to be honest with victims at all stages of the process by explaining what the criminal justice system can and cannot do, and by clarifying that they represent the state, not the legal interests of victims. They should prepare victims to understand the limited role they play in a criminal trial. This is particularly important when a victim's testimony leads to one conclusion, and DNA or other forensic evidence leads to another. Prosecutors, working with victim advocates, can help victims understand that human memory is not always perfect.

In a similar vein, prosecutors have a special obligation to victims when new evidence emerges to reopen an investigation the victim thought was closed. A hit in a cold case, or exoneration by DNA evidence in a case where the victim's testimony had led to a conviction, can produce great emotional turmoil. In these circumstances, prosecutors and victim advocates should take special care to assist victims and offer counseling and understanding.

In many states, prosecutors have a legal obligation to confer with victims at various stages of the criminal justice process. However, in an environment where prosecutors believe that their first responsibility is to build strong cases, argue issues with defense counsel, and respond to the concerns of the presiding judge, victims' interests are often disregarded. This is unfortunate because victims' concerns are often relevant to the proceedings, particularly when they have ongoing fear for their safety. Prosecutors should bring these issues to the attention of the court to influence judges' decisions regarding bail conditions, pleas, and sentencing.

In many instances, however, the criminal justice process cannot meet the needs of crime victims. Nonetheless, Parallel Justice requires prosecutors to respond to victims in new ways. As representatives of the state, and the highest elected law enforcement officials, prosecutors should define their duty to seek justice broadly to include providing justice to victims. Accordingly, prosecutors should find opportunities to communicate directly to victims that what happened to them was wrong and that they will do everything they can to help.

Charles Hynes, district attorney of Brooklyn, New York, and vice-president of the National District Attorneys Association, has taken a number of steps consistent with Parallel Justice principles. He recently revised his Web site to create a special section providing guidance and resources for victims of crime. For those involved in cases handled by his office, DA Hynes sends a letter containing four messages. First, the letter explains victims' rights in New York State. Second, it describes the victim compensation program. Third, it explains the assistance available from the victim services unit in his office. But perhaps most important, the letter begins with the statement "What happened to you was wrong, and I want you to know my staff will do everything it can to assist you." By speaking in this voice, and acknowledging the harm caused by the crime, prosecutors can underscore the communal commitment to crime victims that is at the heart of Parallel Justice.

As is set forth in detail below, the tenets of Parallel Justice require that prosecutors make three commitments to crime victims: to make their safety a high priority, to implement their rights within the criminal justice system, and to inform them of their rights to pursue justice in the civil courts.

Make Victim Safety a High Priority

Beginning with the first conversation with a crime victim and continuing throughout the case, prosecutors should inquire whether victims are safe and, if not, what their specific concerns are. For example, prosecutors should ascertain whether victims are being intimidated or harassed by an offender or his associates. They should ask whether victims feel safe at home and at work. All information regarding safety should be considered when arguing for bail and recommending a particular sentence. In some cases, a victim's safety concerns might influence the fundamental decision whether to prosecute the case at all.

The following examples illustrate the relevance of these safety considerations to the exercise of prosecutorial discretion. In a bail argument, the prosecutor should inform the court if the victim fears retaliation and does not feel safe at home. In such a case, a prosecutor might argue for a higher bail and/or an order of protection. The same process of consultation and recommendations to the court should be followed during plea negotiations and sentencing. For example, a sentence might include a stay-away order, revocation of a gun license, or protection of third parties such as the victim's children. Finally, a prosecutor's decision whether to divert a particular case from prosecution, or dismiss it, should be influenced by whether a victim feels threatened, and continuing court supervision of the offender is more likely to avoid further harm.

A prosecutor recognizing an ongoing relationship that threatens a victim's safety can work with victim advocates and engage the victim in safety planning. In addition to other strategies, this process would include providing information about orders of protection—where and how to obtain such orders, their strengths and limitations, and the process for enforcing them. In cases of severe intimidation, victims should be offered protection and relocation services. In the few local jurisdictions where witness protection services are now available, they are typically limited to cases involving gangs or organized crime. But many other categories of victims fear for their safety, including victims of intimate partner violence, hate crime, stalking, elder abuse, sexual assault, as well as the crime of witness intimidation. Parallel Justice supports assistance for all victims who fear for their safety, regardless of the nature of the crime. Furthermore, since the danger to the victim may not disappear when a criminal prosecution is completed, the obligation to provide safety to victims should not automatically end when a case is closed.

Prosecutors should also consider victims' safety when determining whether a victim should testify. Understandably, many victims fear participation in the criminal justice process, so prosecutors should make every effort to find other evidence to allow a prosecution to go forward rather than compel testimony. If there are ongoing safety concerns, victim/witness protection services should be offered, whether or not the prosecutor has decided to ask the victim to testify.

Implement Victims' Rights

Most victims' rights legislation imposes obligations on prosecutors. For example, under the typical statutory framework, prosecutors must notify victims of all critical stages in the criminal justice process, confer with victims before a plea agreement, and inform them of their rights to attend proceedings and to enter a victim impact statement at the time of sentencing.

Unfortunately, as is outlined in chapter 2, these laws are often not followed. Blatant and consistent disregard for the law is deeply troubling and perplexing to many victims. One of the most important ways that prosecutors can secure justice for victims is to follow the law and ensure that victims can exercise their rights.

Victims' rights must be implemented even when the views of the victim do not coincide with those of the prosecutor. For example, in every state, victims have a right to speak or to submit a written victim impact statement at sentencing. The prosecutor must notify the victim of this right, even if the victim's views do not coincide with the prosecutor's recommendation on sentencing. Failure to do so undermines victims' confidence in the criminal justice system, deprives the court of useful information, and makes victims' future participation less likely.

Inform Victims of Their Rights to Civil Justice

Within the Parallel Justice framework, prosecutors have an obligation to make every effort to ensure that victims of crime benefit from all avenues to justice, including their right to pursue justice through the civil courts. Civil justice offers a very robust set of legal options that are rarely known or understood by crime victims. Prosecutors can explain that almost every crime is also a tort, which a crime victim can litigate as a plaintiff in civil court, where the victim's interests can be represented.

For example, while the state may prosecute an offender in criminal court for assault, he or she may also be held accountable to the victim for the same assault in civil court. Victims may also pursue actions against third parties whose negligence contributed to the crime. For example, a rape victim might sue not only the rapist but also the hotel where the rape occurred if the hotel failed to provide adequate security. Civil litigation requires a lower standard of proof than a criminal trial, so evidence that is insufficient to prove guilt beyond a reasonable doubt and sustain a criminal conviction may be sufficient to meet the standard of a preponderance of evidence, leading to a finding of civil liability.

Crime victims pursue civil justice for many reasons. For some, it is an opportunity to recover damages. For others, it provides a chance to obtain more information about the crime through discovery. Some victims choose civil justice to have more control over the proceedings than the criminal justice process offers. Many crime victims hope that establishing civil liability and imposing penalties on the offender or other liable parties will make it less likely others will suffer similar crimes. Other victims simply want to "have their day in court."

Prosecutors could play a new and significant role in helping victims rebuild their lives by informing them of the existence of the civil justice system. Meeting this obligation could be as easy as giving victims a brochure explaining the civil justice system, and listing contact information for legal referral services.

THE COURTS

How a criminal court judge conducts a trial and interacts with victims can tip the balance from a painful and alienating experience to one that leaves the victim, regardless of the outcome, feeling heard, and having greater trust in the process. A judge's obligations toward victims resemble those of the police and the prosecutor. Judges should ensure that the safety of the victim is considered throughout the proceedings. In appropriate circumstances, judges should determine whether a victim's safety is compromised by testifying, or whether an order of protection should be issued. Judges should also do their part in implementing victims' rights to be notified of critical proceedings, to be present, and to participate. In most states, victims also have a right to have restitution considered, a right that judges should enforce. Finally, like all other participants in the criminal justice system, judges should treat victims with dignity and respect.

At sentencing, when victims appear in court to enter a victim impact statement, judges should explain the limited purpose of a victim impact statement, that this statement is but one of many factors that will be considered in deciding the sentence, and that their statement alone will not determine the sentence. Victims should know that, under our system of criminal justice, they do not have that power, nor do they have to carry that burden.

Because it is often difficult for victims to testify about the impact of the crime, and because reliving the experience can be painful, even traumatic, it would be helpful for judges to express their appreciation to victims for coming to court, acknowledge the difficulty involved, and be respectful throughout their testimony.

Judicial obligations exist independently of the prosecutor's obligations. In other words, Parallel Justice encourages judges to make a separate inquiry regarding whether victims are safe, even if prosecutors have not raised the issue in court. Similarly, Parallel Justice supports judges' asking victims directly whether prosecutors have informed them of their rights. One way to accomplish this would be for judges to refer to a checklist of all the victims' rights that are relevant to a prosecution, and to ask if these rights have been implemented. In so doing, judges would continually remind prosecutors of their obligations to victims, and demonstrate to victims that their rights are important.

PROBATION, PAROLE, AND CORRECTIONS

Three criminal justice agencies —probation, parole, and corrections—have extensive contact with people convicted of crimes, and therefore have unique opportunities to advance the aims of Parallel Justice. These agencies should all support sentences, programs, and opportunities that will increase the likelihood that offenders will do no further harm, acknowledge responsibility for their actions, and pay restitution. Probation, parole, and corrections agencies should also enforce victims' rights, treat victims with respect and sensitivity, and participate in a comprehensive communal response to assist victims. Finally, because such a large portion of the individuals in their caseloads or their custody are themselves victims of crime, they also have an obligation to provide these individuals with appropriate services.

Make Victim Safety A Priority

From the initial interview to prepare a pre-sentence report, to a victim's statement at a parole hearing, corrections officials should be particularly focused on safety concerns. When victims are living in fear, probation, corrections, and parole officials should take steps to help prevent repeat victimization. When appropriate, they should counsel victims about the importance of safety planning and the availability of orders of protection, then create plans to ensure those orders are not violated. This information should factor into discharge decisions and conditions of release such requiring mental health treatment or electronic surveillance, or specifying "zones of safety" for victims. Like police and prosecutors, officials in corrections, probation, and parole agencies should refer victims to victim advocates for assistance with safety planning, practical support, and counseling.

In recent years, corrections, probation, and parole agencies have all developed innovative programs designed to promote successful reintegration of offenders. These agencies should also ensure that any services provided to offenders, or conditions of release designed to promote offender reintegration, do not conflict with the safety needs of victims. For example, if a victim has an order of protection stating that the offender must stay away from the victim's home and place of employment, the offender should not participate in drug rehabilitation, job training, or transitional housing at times and locations that would violate such an order. At a minimum, offender reintegration plans should not place victims at risk of further harm.

According to parole and prisoner reentry expert Joan Petersilia, "Arguably, crime victims are the people who are most affected by the return of over 600,000 inmates each year, and we must consider their salient needs and concerns."[10] A few states have begun to incorporate "victim wraparound" sessions into their prisoner reentry procedures. Two states, Washington and Vermont, emphasize particularly broad-based community support for victims in their wraparound meetings. Working with corrections officials, victims are asked to think through their safety and emotional needs when the offender is released from prison, and encouraged to develop ways that others in the community—ranging from law enforcement and probation or parole officers to family and friends, employers, members of the clergy, and neighbors—can take concrete actions to address these needs. This kind of corrections-based, victim-oriented program, comparable to the "cocoons" police can initiate, reflects an understanding that the goals of successful prisoner reentry and victim safety are frequently aligned.

While many victims fear the return of offenders into their communities, they have a strong interest in reentry initiatives designed to prevent recidivism. Thus it makes good sense for corrections agencies to ensure the participation of victims and victims' organizations in reentry planning.[11]

Corrections officials should also find opportunities to tell victims that they believe what happened to them was wrong, and that they will help them in any way possible. In Orange County, New York, following a workshop on Parallel Justice, a probation officer sent a form letter to a victim explaining that the victim had an opportunity to offer a victim impact statement at the time of sentencing. Before mailing the letter, the officer added a handwritten message, "What happened to you was wrong. I am here to assist you in any way I can." Immediately upon receiving the letter, the victim called the officer to say that nobody, up until that point, had acknowledged that fact, and she felt so much better. Solely because of this message she decided to offer a victim impact statement. After this experience the Orange County Probation Department decided to rework all of its correspondence to victims.

Implement Victims' Rights

In most states, victims' rights laws obligate corrections departments to inform crime victims when the individual convicted of harming them is about to be released. Some laws also require notification of any change in a prisoner's location during the period of incarceration. These statutory obligations typically apply only in instances where victims affirmatively indicate they want this information.[12] The "opt-in" characteristic of this particular victim's right places an important obligation on prosecutors, courts, and corrections agencies to let victims know they are entitled to this notification. Ideally, victims would not need to state an affirmative desire for notification, but rather could "opt-out" if, for example, they no longer want to be reminded of the crime.

Automated notification procedures, which now exist in some form in almost every state, make it increasingly simple to implement this right. These systems provide a twenty-four-hour service for victims to call for information regarding a prisoner's location and release dates, and to receive electronic notification when a release date approaches or any other change in a prisoner's status occurs.

Notification of a prisoner's impending release can be critical to victims who need to prepare themselves emotionally, and/or take steps to protect themselves. As the release date approaches, corrections departments should communicate directly with victims, inquiring what their needs are, whether they fear for their safety, and, when appropriate, engage them in safety planning. They should also work with local police departments and parole agencies when threats to victim safety require a law enforcement response. Corrections departments can either develop the internal capacity to work with victims on safety planning, or refer victims to community-based victim services for that assistance and other forms of counseling.[13]

Promote Responsibility and Enforce Restitution Awards

Too often, our criminal justice process sidesteps the issue of responsibility, or creates artificial constructs in the name of accountability that are meaningless to crime victims. For example, many diversion programs require that a participant acknowledge culpability for wrongdoing, but this is never conveyed to the victim. Typically, guilty pleas in a courtroom are rituals lacking any human dimension. Often the plea bears little relationship to the events experienced by the victim. Expressions of remorse at parole hearings can be quite genuine, but can also seem to be play-acting performed to increase the likelihood of early release.

In an adversarial system that tends to polarize victims and offenders, and in practice often discourages truth-telling, it is difficult to promote genuine acknowledgments of responsibility. Even so, probation, parole, and corrections agencies can foster responsibility in a number of ways, often through communication with victims. Some victims want face-to-face or written communication with the person who committed the crime against them. They should be given such opportunities through a safe and supportive process. Victim advocates should prepare both victims and offenders for these encounters, to ensure that their expectations are realistic and that they are emotionally ready to hear what the other party might say.

A number of more formal mechanisms also involve direct communication between victims and offenders. Victim Offender Reconciliation Panels (VORP), which provide a facilitated forum for victims and offenders to meet, talk about the crime and its impact, and move toward some measure of reconciliation, have a long-standing acceptance in some correctional systems. Furthermore, as discussed in chapter 2, a wide variety of restorative justice programs have also been developed in this country. Some are community-based; others operate within the criminal justice system. All emphasize healing through direct communication among victims, offenders, and members of their respective communities, and all have great potential for those victims and offenders who want to participate in them.

Other methods of sharing information and promoting responsibility do not involve direct communication between victims and offenders. For example, many correctional agencies have implemented victim impact panels, in which crime victims—not the victims of the offenders in the room, but representative victims—talk with offenders about how their lives have been changed as a result of the crime. These panels, designed to foster empathy, are usually geared to individuals convicted of drunk driving or sexual assault, and could easily be expanded to other kinds of crime.

Several states have developed curricula designed to help prisoners understand and take responsibility for their actions. Some programs, such as Resolve to Stop the Violence (RSVP) in San Francisco involve a significant amount of victim participation, others do not. Recently, the Osborne Association in New York City, working with a task force of academics, defense attorneys, victim advocates, and formerly incarcerated individuals, developed a curriculum on individual responsibility for incarcerated people, called "Coming to Terms." The objective of this sixteen-week course is to explore the issue of responsibility in the context of a profoundly personal journey traveled by individual participants. To create an environment where people can speak freely, the course will be taught by non-correctional staff. Participants will be encouraged to reflect on their lives, take responsibility for their actions, acknowledge the harm that resulted from their crimes, understand remorse, and develop ways to make positive contributions to society. The curriculum will soon be offered to a group of individuals in the New York State prison system serving long sentences for violent crimes. For some victims, knowing that the individual who harmed them has "come to terms" with the consequences of his actions will be enormously gratifying. Similar curricula that challenge and support participants through a complex personal process should be created for people on probation and parole.

Participation in such programs, or other experiences in prison, on probation, or on parole, can sometimes lead to a desire to apologize to a victim. These agencies should develop policies and practices to ensure that people under their supervision are never forced to apologize, never expect to benefit from doing so, but do understand how to make an apology as meaningful as possible.[14] Parallel Justice principles promote apologies with four components very similar to those advocated by restorative justice practitioners: 1) a clear statement of responsibility for actions constituting the crime and that those actions were wrong; 2) an acknowledgment of the impact the crime has had on the victim; 3) a statement of regret; and 4) a commitment to do no further harm.[15]

Responsibility can also be promoted in the context of community corrections. For example, it is now a common judicial practice to order community service as part of a sentence. Whenever possible, the service should benefit victims. In Bend, Oregon, in a program created by Dennis Maloney, the county's Department of Community Justice (formerly the Department of Probation) arranges for people on probation to repair victims' property, construct housing for battered women, and run routine errands for crime victims. While individual offenders may not address the needs of the victims of their specific crimes, they assist other victims, and contribute to the communal response to victims. In light of the research showing that offenders who pay restitution are less likely to recidivate than those who do not, these community service projects, which provide indirect restitution to crime victims, may also reduce future criminal behavior. As this model is replicated across the country through Civic Justice Corps initiatives, it is particularly important to retain the emphasis on service to victims found in the original Deschutes County program.

Corrections agencies should also reinforce the importance of offenders' paying restitution to victims, for at least three reasons. First, court orders should not be ignored. Second, restitution matters a great deal to victims. Third, payment of restitution is associated with decreased rates of recidivism.[16] If these agencies took these obligations seriously, the results would be profound, as victims would feel that the criminal justice system took their experiences seriously and was doing its part in keeping them safe and helping them rebuild their lives.

Provide Assistance

Finally, as was set forth in chapter 1, a high percentage of all incarcerated people, and an even higher percentage of incarcerated females, have been victims of violence before entering the prison system.[17] Many more become victims of crime while in prison. Thus corrections departments have a unique opportunity to address the impact of those crimes. Such assistance will require a fundamental realignment of policies and practice. Corrections staff should be required, and funded, to assess the long-term consequences of prior victimization, and provide necessary counseling and support services.

The issue of crime within prisons, just as in many other controlled environments, such as the military, mental institutions, or college campuses, is complex. On the one hand, there are notorious incidents of severe crimes in prisons that have not been brought to the attention of police and prosecutors. Clearly, ignoring these crimes, or handling them solely through internal disciplinary procedures, is inappropriate when the harms are significant. On the other hand, not every act that is technically a crime can or should be prosecuted. What is important, however, is that local police and prosecutors work with corrections officials to create clear and transparent guidelines as to how to respond to crimes committed in prisons.

In all instances, consistent with Parallel Justice principles, when a crime is committed in a prison, the victim of that crime should have access to victim services. Corrections agencies should either develop the internal capacity, or partner with local victim service providers, to offer these victims counseling, appropriate treatment, and safety planning to prevent repeat victimization. In many cases, this will require victim service providers to rethink their service delivery models. This will also require funders, including some legislatures, to lift restrictions that exclude prisoners from eligibility for government-funded victim services. For example, the state of New Hampshire recently passed legislation, introduced by long-time victim advocate State Representative Renny Cushing, extending eligibility for victim compensation to prisoners.[18] Consistent with Parallel Justice, these victims of crime are entitled to be treated as all crime victims should be.

The recently enacted federal Prison Rape Elimination Act has focused national attention on the high number of rapes and other sexual assaults occurring in prisons, and the profound impact these crimes have on their victims. A landmark national study was commissioned to document the incidence of rape in prison, requiring corrections departments nationwide to report sexual violence inside their walls. This clearly represents important progress, but we should do much more than document the incidence of rape in prison; we should provide help for the victims of these rapes, just as we would for any other victims of sexual assault. Corrections departments should strive to address the impact of victimization both prior to, and during, imprisonment.

VICTIM ADVOCATES

All criminal justice agencies, from the police through corrections, probation, and parole, should employ victim advocates to help victims through the maze and the emotional turmoil of the criminal justice process. These advocates can communicate regularly with victims, give them information about each stage in the process, ensure that they understand their legal rights, and make efforts to keep victims' safety and rights a high priority within their respective agencies. They can also help victims access other services and resources in the community.

While advocates based in the criminal justice system are constrained by the overarching goals of their agencies (which are not primarily focused on victims), designating someone to focus exclusively on victims, listen to their concerns, and advocate for them within the context of the criminal justice system, can be enormously helpful to victims. In addition, these advocates tend to hear firsthand accounts of victims' experiences with other professionals throughout their agencies, and thus can help determine whether agencies' policies and practices are consistent with Parallel Justice, and their operations aligned to serve victims well.

Community-based advocates often have more flexibility in how they approach their work because they are able to focus exclusively on victims' needs without regard to the offender-oriented interests and time pressures of the criminal justice process. As a result, these advocates are often better suited to ask victims to describe the full range of their crime-related needs, and work with them to determine the best ways to address them. While system-based services are usually limited to the duration of the offender's case in the system, community-based services can be accessed whenever they are needed, and typically include a wider range of resources and assistance. In addition to information and emotional support as victims go through the criminal justice process, community-based advocates may offer individual and group counseling, assistance with food, clothing, and shelter, safety planning, advocacy to employers, landlords, public assistance and other social service agencies, employment counseling, and referrals to additional resources.

Parallel Justice initiatives challenge all victim advocates, wherever they are based, to find new ways to raise public awareness about the far-reaching impact of crime, to extend their reach to help many more victims, and to develop a wide variety of creative partnerships with public and private organizations. Victim advocates are particularly well suited to understand the issues that all victims of crime have in common. They can argue persuasively that it is counterproductive to create categories of victims that perpetuate needless hierarchies. Advocates appreciate that victims of economic or property crime often experience trauma and hardship similar to that experienced by victims of violent crime. They understand that all victims who fear for their safety—regardless of the underlying crime—need protection. Garnering support for Parallel Justice will enable advocates to create greater public awareness about the common ground shared by all victims of crime, and how important it is to address the emotional, physical, and financial needs of every individual victim rather than limit services and resources to categories of victims. Advocates are also in a unique position to help policymakers understand how important it is for all victims to have the opportunity to observe and participate in the criminal justice process.

Parallel Justice also encourages victim advocates to emphasize preventing repeat victimization. Research demonstrates that all crime victims, not just battered women and victims of sexual assault, should be assisted in developing plans that reduce the likelihood of another crime. Victim advocates are trained to assess the best time to have these conversations, as well as to help victims understand that while they are not responsible for the crime committed against them, they can take steps to be less vulnerable.

Further, advocates are especially aware of the importance of reaching victims who are particularly vulnerable to crime: teenagers, people living in low-income communities, and those who are in prison, mental institutions, nursing homes, or homeless shelters. Similarly, for victims who do not speak English, are physically or mentally challenged, are illiterate, or are too poor to travel to a service provider, advocates must develop different strategies to ensure access to assistance. Parallel Justice supports creative partnerships between victim service providers and government and community-based agencies to assist all victims of crime, with particular attention to those who remain underserved or completely invisible.

In most communities, if there are any system-based victim services, they are typically limited to crisis intervention, and support for victims of violent crime as they go through the criminal justice process—if the offender has been identified and will be prosecuted. Community-based services are often available only to victims of sexual assault and domestic violence. Parallel Justice, however, requires us to respond to the full range of immediate and ongoing needs of all victims of any kind of crime. Generally, it is not feasible for victim service providers to expand their efforts to meet all of these needs. Instead, advocates can continue to forge creative partnerships with agencies and organizations who haven't traditionally served crime victims.

Some communities have developed particularly successful multi-agency initiatives and co-located services for victims. For instance, through both federal and local government support, several cities have created Family Justice Centers where victims of domestic violence can access traditional victim services from several nonprofit organizations, see police, prosecutors, and probation officers, and also meet with representatives from public assistance, employment, and housing agencies all at one location. Initiatives such as these, which coordinate services through case management and facilitate access to a broad range of services, should be expanded to include victims of any kind of crime.

Creative partnerships can also provide significant new resources to assist crime victims. For example, to extend its reach, the National Center for Victims of Crime partnered with the American Automobile Association to distribute information about what people should do when they become victims of crime while traveling. Similarly, in collaboration with The Enterprise Foundation, a leading developer of low-income housing, local community development corporations, and district attorneys from several cities, the National Center designed a range of relocation options for intimidated victims and witnesses. In order to reach adolescent victims of crime, the National Center partnered with local youth development organizations such as Boys and Girls Clubs, a YMCA, and a middle school to launch Teen Victim Projects in selected communities. At the national level, the National Crime Prevention Council joined the collaboration to create teen-oriented outreach strategies. These projects represent successful efforts to find common ground with other agencies — in one case the safety of travelers, another, the safety of witnesses, and finally, the healthy development of adolescents — in order to help victims of crime more effectively than through traditional victim services alone.

When a community embraces the ideal of Parallel Justice, victim advocates and service providers should welcome the participation of residents, businesses, and community-based organizations, and help them find the most appropriate ways to contribute. Grounded in direct experience with victims, advocates and service providers can identify the most useful ways for every member of a community to participate in a Parallel Justice effort. These partnerships will enable victim service providers to assist more victims of crime than they ever could on their own.

In addition to partnering with other sectors of society, victim advocates can bring victims' interests into general policy debates about crime, criminal justice, healthcare, and social services. For example, advocates should represent victims' needs and concerns as new emergency room policies are debated in local hospitals, and as criminal justice practitioners discuss police priorities, alternatives to incarceration, reentry planning, or DNA testing backlogs. And victims' interests should be considered when social service priorities (e.g., regarding housing, daycare, job training, and literacy) are reviewed. By engaging victim advocates, a wide range of professionals will better understand the concerns of crime victims, and will be more likely to resolve policy debates in ways that benefit victims.

HEALTHCARE

Second only to law enforcement, the healthcare system, and hospitals in particular, represent the service sector most likely to encounter crime victims in crisis. While healthcare providers are legally required to report certain injuries to the police, their responsibility to victims often ends there. Consistent with the principles of Parallel Justice, doctors and nurses have an obligation not only to treat the immediate presenting problem but also to address the ongoing health and safety needs of the patient/victim. It is important to identify a victim of an assault, not just a broken bone, and to see a victim of an attempted murder, not just a knife wound.

A number of examples demonstrate different approaches to tapping the assistance of healthcare providers. For example, recognizing the important role healthcare providers play in society's response to victims of crime, the state of Pennsylvania enacted a law requiring hospital staff to identify patients who were domestic violence victims and refer them to victim services.[19] And, as part of the Parallel Justice initiative in Redlands, California, a local hospital's camp for children who have lost parents to illness expanded to include children who lost parents to violence.

The Shock Trauma Center at the University of Maryland Medical Center took a more comprehensive approach and developed the successful Violence Intervention Program (VIP), whose goal is to reduce the number of patients/victims who return to the hospital with injuries from intentional violence such as gunshots, beatings, and stabbings. Patients who participate in VIP are counseled about the likelihood of the violence continuing, and engaged in discussion about how to stay safe in the future. Patients meet with a case manager, and if relevant, a parole or probation officer, to create an intervention plan consisting of services such as substance abuse treatment, employment training, housing, and education. After patients are discharged from the hospital, home visits and weekly counseling continues. An evaluation of VIP showed that participants were not only 7 times less likely to be readmitted for violent injuries, they were also 3 times less likely to be re-arrested for a violent crime.

According to Dr. Cornell Cooper, founder of VIP and Associate Professor of Surgery at the University of Maryland School of Medicine, the benefits extended far beyond the reduction in violence. "Our study shows that the VIP has had a broader impact than we ever imagined it would. Our original goal was simply to reduce the number of patients re-admitted to Shock Trauma because of violent injuries. Not only have we achieved that goal, but we are also seeing less criminal activity among our program participants, as well as families being reunited, fathers getting jobs, paying taxes, and paying child support. It's turned out to be a very cost-effective program overall."[20]

This approach to healthcare is consistent with the concept of Parallel Justice because it recognizes the primacy of safety planning, helps victims recover from the trauma of the crime by taking more control over their lives, and provides real options for victims to consider as they move forward.

Though victims may not want to relive the crime by describing what happened to them, healthcare professionals can be sensitive as they obtain information about injuries consistent with violence or neglect. Asking direct questions gives patients/victims permission to talk about events that can be shaming and stigmatizing, and takes the onus off those who may want information but are afraid to ask for it.

Not naming the violence that caused the injury, and not talking to victims about safety planning or referring them to victim advocates for assistance, adds to their risk of future violence and injury. And, just as healthcare professionals provide information about the long-term effects of any injury or illness, they should also inform victims of likely emotional or psychological problems they might experience as a result of the crime-related trauma, and direct them to the appropriate resources.

Following the Parallel Justice framework, this approach to healthcare sends a message to victims that their experiences matter to these professionals (and by extension, to society), and that these professionals will do what they can, not only to help them heal their wounds but also to prevent further injury. Ignoring the obvious causes of illness or injury, or failing to acknowledge that patients were victims of violence, can be just as harmful to victims' well-being as the experience of police, prosecutors, or judges trivializing the violence or harm victims have suffered.

SOCIAL SERVICES

By participating in a comprehensive communal response, social service providers can help victims stay safe, recover from the trauma of crime, and access critical resources and services. As discussed in chapter 3, many crime victims need services, resources, and practical assistance, beyond the capacity of local victim services. Social service agencies should partner with victim service providers to maximize access to services that would benefit victims of crime.

Some victims, in crime's wake, suddenly feel unsafe in their homes or communities, and need to relocate to a different community and find new housing. Some need to find new jobs or even develop new work skills. Some need emergency daycare while they attend court, go to counseling, or take a new job. Some victims' psychological needs go beyond the capacity of crisis intervention or victim support groups to help. These victims may need short- or long-term psychological therapy. Victims who use drugs or alcohol to cope with the trauma of crime may need substance-abuse treatment. Whenever possible, consistent with Parallel Justice, social service agencies should make special allowances to give priority to victims of crime.

Social service agencies may discover that some of the clients they are already serving are also victims of crime at risk for revictimization, suffering from posttraumatic stress, or facing new challenges because of crime-related disability. For instance, appointments may need to change at the last minute as these victims juggle meetings with criminal justice officials, or adjust their schedules to accommodate a host of new, crime-related activities. Some victims may feel disoriented after experiencing the trauma of a crime, and may need special assistance with forms or paperwork. Victims of car crashes caused by drunk driving, victims whose cars have been stolen, or those suffering physical injuries from other crimes, may arrive late to appointments for a while as they get used to using new methods of transportation. Crime victims should be able to access the full range of social services offered by their communities, knowing that their experiences as victims of crime will be taken into account by social service professionals who will tailor services to their needs, and provide appropriate referrals for support services and counseling.

All social service agencies, including those that provide some of the most basic services such as public housing, food stamps, or public assistance, should be encouraged to treat victims of crime with respect and compassion, tell them that what happened to them was wrong, make special allowances when appropriate, provide all the assistance they can, and refer victims to more specialized services whenever necessary.

EMPLOYERS

Employers can also take part in a Parallel Justice response by supporting employees who have been victims of crime. Enabling victims to take time off to meet with police or go to court, seek crime-related counseling or other services, or apply for victim compensation sends a powerful and supportive message to all employees. For those who don't feel safe in the workplace, employers should offer to post photographs of people who have been mandated to stay away from them, change their work schedules, telephone extensions, and e-mail addresses, escort them to their method of transportation home, or move them to another location. In addition, employer-provided insurance benefits that cover mental health services should include helping victims obtain appropriate assistance. Employers can also ensure that employee assistance programs offer counseling appropriate to crime victims, delivered by professionals trained in the dynamics of trauma.

BUSINESSES

Businesses can support Parallel Justice by helping victims in their communities in a variety of creative ways. For example, businesses could designate a percentage of their resources as free or discounted products or services for crime victims, such as materials and labor to repair property damage, and new locks or windows for burglary victims. Stores and restaurants could donate gift certificates. Unused food from restaurants, clothes and toiletries discarded by hotels, and furniture and kitchen supplies no longer needed at department stores, could be made available for victims in emergency and transitional housing. Healthcare professionals could provide physical therapy, dental work, and reconstructive surgery pro bono. Beauty salons could offer treatments to help assault victims look and feel better. Toy stores could donate products to help child victims recover from the trauma of losing their own toys because of sudden relocation, theft, or arson. Accountants could offer to help prepare tax returns for victims too overwhelmed to focus on the forms. The list is endless.

Any business that provides a product or service has something of value to offer, and can contribute to the communal response to help victims get their lives back on track. Parallel Justice business initiatives can be organized through partnerships between local chambers of commerce and victim advocates and/or any other government, civic, or community-based agency that wants to coordinate the effort.

The Parallel Justice initiative in Burlington, Vermont, features a resource bank through which victims receive small amounts of money, goods, or services for crime-related expenses not covered by victim compensation. For example, one victim whose car had been vandalized was given $250 to meet his insurance deductible so he could have his car repaired. Burlington's business community has supported the resource bank by donating or discounting a wide range of products and services. A few examples: The Acme Glass Company donated all labor associated with repairing broken windows for crime victims. The Ski Rack store offered an 8 percent discount to victims who bought new bicycles to replace ones that were stolen, and a free new lock as well. A certified daycare provider donated free emergency daycare for victims. Some businesses contributed goods or services to address life's necessities, while others have donated items such as free pedicures, movie tickets, or meals in restaurants, to demonstrate community concern for victims' well-being.

Victim compensation programs might reimburse victims for some of these expenses, but many victims cannot afford to spend their own money and then wait weeks or months for compensation. Where compensation is ultimately available, and outright donations are not feasible, the private sector can try to work out arrangements with the state's victim compensation board, under which businesses make products or services available for crime victims when they are needed, and secure repayment for their expenses at a later date.

Finally, businesses can help victims by providing financial support to victim service providers or by funding local Parallel Justice initiatives such as a resource bank, a victimization survey, or a public awareness campaign.

Neighbors, Friends, and Family

Parallel Justice envisions an obligation and an opportunity for all of us as neighbors, friends, and family, to respond to victims with sensitivity and compassion, and whenever possible to help them continue to have positive relationships with others. Crime rips at the fabric of communities in many ways. It can cause victims to feel disoriented, grow distrustful, and ultimately become isolated. Some develop new fears and vulnerabilities that are hard to communicate and difficult to resolve. Sensing that others may not understand or care about what they have been through, crime victims often withdraw from community life.

Depending on the nature of the crime, and victims' reactions, it can be difficult for victims to relate to friends and family members as they did before. They may feel embarrassed or ashamed, and blame themselves or fear that others will. They may be confused or angry. Victims often experience a wide range of emotions, which in itself can be disorienting. Sometimes, the cruelty of crime may be almost paralyzing for both the victim and people in the immediate community who are also dealing with the shock. Coupled with the insensitivity to victims' needs frequently exhibited by first responders such as police officers, doctors, nurses, or social workers, victims' lack of trust and sense of isolation are likely to be reinforced.

When someone experiences a death in the family, friends and neighbors usually think of ways to be helpful, shopping for food and cooking meals, taking turns with child-care, and helping with other chores. When someone is sick, neighbors often express concern and offer emotional support, companionship, and help in keeping up with responsibilities. When a home is destroyed by fire or a flood, family members and friends are quick to offer food, clothing, shelter, and all sorts of practical assistance. In these times of personal hardship, it is not only the assistance that makes a difference; it is the human contact, the concern, and the compassion that are communicated.

Many people are not as comfortable responding in similar ways to victims of crime. Some people feel awkward, hesitant to acknowledge that a crime has occurred for fear of breaching privacy or reopening emotional wounds. Others just do not realize how traumatic the experience of crime can be, and therefore it does not occur to them to offer the same kinds of assistance.

Families, friends, and neighbors, however, can make a significant contribution to the communal response by working together to focus on the safety of the victim and help prevent repeat victimization. As described earlier in this chapter, at the request of a victim and in collaboration with law enforcement efforts, community members can create "cocoons" around victims to watch for and report certain activities that may endanger them.

Neighbors, friends, and family can also relieve victims of some of their routine responsibilities so they can more easily manage new challenges they face in the aftermath of crime. Neighbors, friends, and family can help transport victims who need to speak with police investigators or a prosecutor, or attend court. They can help with home repairs after a break-in, or help replace damaged or stolen items. For example, the friends of a woman whose jewelry had been stolen each gave her an item from their own jewelry boxes. Caring for children or elderly parents, cooking meals, doing yard work, feeding pets, or helping with the paperwork required to apply for victim compensation are all meaningful ways to help.

Often, support comes in the simplest forms: sharing a cup of coffee, accompanying victims to court or to appointments, and being willing to listen without judgment or giving advice can make an enormous difference in a crime victim's sense of connection to others. With each gesture, neighbors, friends, and family help repair the fabric of community life.

During a workshop on Parallel Justice in Vermont, one of the participants coined the phrase "Casserole Justice" to capture this notion of individuals "doing the right thing" and joining the communal response to victims of crime. Though we often rely on individual initiative, these efforts can be organized by neighbors, faith institutions, block associations, or civic groups. Some victims will not want any of this assistance because it feels better to regain their equilibrium on their own. Even so, when community members acknowledge that what happened was wrong, express concern, and offer support, it is usually enormously appreciated, and both the victim and the community are better off.

Legislators

It is appropriate for victims to look to government, and in particular to their elected officials serving in legislative bodies, to assist them. Previous discussion has identified some roles the legislative branch of government should play. For example, legislators should make every effort to ensure that all victims have legal rights to meaningful engagement in the criminal justice process, and should establish expectations for victims to have respectful and helpful interactions with criminal justice, social service, and healthcare agencies.[21]

As to sentencing policy, legislators should be guided by research that shows that victims' views are as diverse as those of the general public. The common belief that all victims favor harsh penalties is simply not true.[22] Victims do share some concerns regarding sentencing, however, such as enforcement of their right to be heard, the need to consider their safety, and the importance of awarding restitution. These concerns, which are reflected in Parallel Justice principles, should be considered whenever sentencing reforms are debated.

Legislatures should also fund victim assistance initiatives to provide emergency and long term support to victims of any kind of crime. Support must extend to victims typically underserved and those not served at all, such as victims of crime in prisons and other institutions. Legislators should also provide funding for regular victimization surveys and other research efforts to understand the nature and extent of local victimization, and to evaluate the effectiveness of victim assistance programs and other interventions.

A number of states have enacted particularly innovative legislation. For example, in an effort to provide victims employment protection, Illinois established the "Victims Economic Security and Safety Act" entitling victims of domestic abuse, sexual violence, or stalking to take up to twelve work weeks of leave, during any twelve-month period, to seek medical attention, obtain services from a victim services organization, obtain psychological or other counseling, participate in safety planning, relocate temporarily or permanently, or seek legal assistance.[23] This kind of employment protection could easily be extended to include victims of any kind of crime who need such assistance.

In order to keep victims safe, the state of Georgia passed legislation authorizing employers to seek a temporary restraining order and injunction on behalf of an employee who has suffered unlawful violence or a credible threat of violence from an individual at the workplace.[24]

These innovative reforms highlight the potential role legislatures can play in promoting the goals of Parallel Justice. In addition to these important reforms, however, there are a number of other, less frequently considered, government functions that should also be realigned with Parallel Justice principles.

Provide Special Allowances

One of the most underdeveloped ways that legislators can help crime victims is to enact laws or encourage policies that reduce the financial burdens victims face in the aftermath of crime. There is no better illustration of the potential for providing tangible financial assistance than the creative and wide-ranging governmental response to the victims of September 11.

Almost immediately after the attacks, as individuals and charitable organizations across the country donated money to support relief efforts, government leaders worked quickly to do their part to lighten the tremendous financial burdens suddenly inflicted on thousands of victims. Early on, the federal government announced that victims of September 11 would get significant federal tax relief and could postpone or reduce payments on federal college loans. The Social Security Administration set up an emergency processing system immediately. In New York, the government waived the one-week waiting period for unemployment insurance claims. The Workers Compensation Board and life insurance companies decided to accept affidavits in lieu of death certificates to expedite the processing of claims. The federal government, through the Department of Labor, created services and temporary jobs for workers temporarily or permanently in need. The government provided equipment and training for victims in transitional employment. And the Federal Emergency Management Agency (FEMA) announced it would cover whatever expenses state victim compensation programs did not cover regarding crisis counseling, funeral expenses, or crime scene cleanup. FEMA also provided low-interest loans or grants for renters and homeowners if their homes were damaged or they were forced to relocate as a result of the attacks.

These creative policy initiatives demonstrated the kinds of special allowances government can and should continue to make for victims of any kind of crime who need financial assistance. We should provide state and federal tax relief for victims who have experienced crime-related financial hardship. We should exclude restitution and death payments from taxable income, and allow victims to deduct all crime-related losses including healthcare and counseling expenses.[25] We should provide debt relief and low-interest loans, as needed, to cover essential living expenses or preexisting financial obligations. The state of Connecticut, for example, even before September 11, began providing low-interest loans up to $100,000 for families of homicide victims.[26] We should also make every effort to expedite victims' access to all government benefits and services, including worker's compensation, unemployment insurance, and Medicaid.

Create Enforcement Mechanisms

Over the last four decades, federal and state legislators have enacted thousands of statutes and state constitutional amendments reflecting a national desire to secure certain legal rights for victims of crime, and government has a clear responsibility to enforce those rights. Few states, however, have provided victims any form of redress or standing to enforce these rights, or imposed any consequences on an agency or official who violates them.[27] Parallel Justice principles create an obligation for all legislators to exercise their authority to make sure these laws are implemented and are not merely hollow promises.

Legislators should exercise their oversight powers to create a culture of accountability among all government agencies. Reporting requirements and oversight hearings can reinforce the message that victims' rights matter, and victims' safety is a government priority. Legislators should also create enforcement mechanisms that encourage victims to report violations of their rights, provide remedies for individual victims whenever possible, and seek solutions to systemic problems. Several states, including South Carolina, Colorado, and Connecticut, have created offices or agencies to investigate and resolve complaints.[28] The form of the enforcement mechanism — an ombudsman, a review committee, or a state advocate — is less important than the authority it has to impose consequences on an offending official. In some states, this authority is limited to issuing reports; in others, legislators have granted authority to reprimand officials and to seek injunctive relief in court on behalf of a victim. Another possibility would be to withhold funding for an agency when there are serious noncompliance problems.

Legislators should also enact laws which give victims legal standing to assert their rights. For example, victims should be able to challenge their exclusion from a criminal trial as it is proceeding. In another context, a victim of harassment, stalking or domestic violence should be able to assert his or her right to prevent government agencies from releasing identifying confidential information. Arizona, Florida, Indiana, and Texas all allow victims to assert their rights in court, while Connecticut allows the state victim advocate to intervene on behalf of a victim during a criminal trial.[29] Whatever the mechanism, the important point here is that legislatures should both create rights for crime victims and the means necessary to enforce them.

Enforce Restitution

When considering the enactment of victims' rights, it is important for legislators to recognize that all rights, not just the right to participate in a criminal trial, need to be enforced. Court orders of restitution are particularly important to victims because they convey a powerful message—that their experience matters to the court, their losses are real, and the offender has an obligation to the victim as well as to the state.

In addition to courts enforcing victims' right to have restitution considered in criminal cases, legislators have an obligation to see that victims get the restitution they are owed. For example, the New York legislature, after determining that district attorneys' offices were not collecting restitution efficiently, passed a law in 1984 requiring each county to designate an entity other than the local district attorney to perform this function. Most counties decided to assign this responsibility to the local probation department. In New York City, however, the Mayor's Office initially split the assignment, and asked the New York City Department of Probation to collect probation-related restitution, and asked the local nonprofit victim services agency, Safe Horizon, to collect restitution in non-probation cases. After twenty years of collecting restitution at a rate consistently higher than the rates of most of the probation departments in counties throughout the state, in 2005, Safe Horizon was asked by the New York City Department of Probation to take over collection of all the restitution cases in the city. This case study underscores the importance of evaluating the effectiveness of restitution collection mechanisms, a function that can be performed well by state legislatures.

Vermont has taken a completely different approach to enforcing orders of restitution. In 2003, the Vermont Legislature added a 15 percent surcharge to criminal and traffic fines and created a restitution fund of $1.2 million in the first year of operation. The state also moved the responsibility for collecting and distributing restitution from the Department of Corrections to the Vermont Center for Crime Victim Services, which created a special restitution unit. Since 2004, whenever restitution is awarded in a case, the unit pays the victim the amount ordered by the court out of the restitution fund, up to a $10,000 cap. The unit then creates an account for each offender, and begins collecting restitution to reimburse the fund.[30] The beauty of this approach is that victims who suffer financial hardship do not have to wait for offenders to pay restitution, and government officials have an added incentive to collect restitution payments owed to the state.

Collecting money owed to the state, however, whether from an award of restitution, overdue parking tickets, taxes, or court-ordered fines, can require sophisticated legal work and a range of tactics from garnishing wages to forfeiture actions. Given the legal expertise these strategies require, and the similarity of tactics across categories of debt, the creation of a single agency, a new Department of Revenue, has recently been discussed in Vermont, and at the time of this writing is under consideration. Should this department become a reality, it would consolidate efforts to collect all money owed the state, including taxes and fines, as well as restitution owed to victims of crime.

VICTIM COMPENSATION

Previous chapters have highlighted both the importance of victim compensation and the shortcomings of our current system. Compensation can make a significant difference in victims' ability to get on with life. Many victims, however, do not know about the availability of compensation, and are not given this information by police or other responders. Many are not eligible to receive compensation, and for those who are eligible, the compensation often does not adequately address their economic losses. In most cases, compensation programs do not consider victims' pain and suffering. Finally, funding for compensation is inappropriately limited to money raised through offender fines and penalties.

Another aspect of our national response to September 11 demonstrated how much better our approach to victim compensation can be. Within days of the attacks, Congress created an unprecedented mechanism to provide federal financial assistance to survivors, the September 11 Victim Compensation Fund (the Fund). Unlike most state victim compensation programs, the availability of the Fund was widely publicized in several languages and through a variety of media. Eligibility was expanded to include unmarried partners who survived a victim, and others designated in a will. Furthermore, victims who had criminal records were not excluded, as they are in many state programs.[31]

The range of losses covered by the Fund was also much more comprehensive than state programs, which cover only short-term expenses, and the most generous programs cap awards at $220,000. By contrast, the Fund, supported by tax dollars, compensated for immediate as well as lifelong economic losses, sometimes totaling millions of dollars per victim. The Fund also covered non-economic losses (pain and suffering), awarding $250,000 per victim in death cases, and another $100,000 for each dependent. For injured victims, there was no cap on awards for non-economic losses.[32]

To be sure, the Fund had its failings. Concerned about lawsuits against the airline industry, Congress offered victims access to the Fund only if they made an unprecedented tradeoff and waived their right to sue the airlines. No state compensation program has a comparable requirement. In addition, the application process was not only overly complicated, but unnecessarily rigid, imposing a short time period within which victims could file. Notwithstanding these shortcomings, the Fund provides a striking example of a generous needs-based approach to victim compensation.

The events of September 11 were unparalleled in many respects, and the nation responded in kind. We may not be able to afford to reimburse victims of everyday crime at the same level as victims of the September 11 attacks, but the Fund demonstrated ways to reach many more victims, and overcome many of the shortcomings of state compensation programs. A number of states are finding new ways to extend their outreach efforts to ensure that more victims are aware of the availability of compensation. For example, for over twenty years, police officers in New York State have been required to give crime victims information about victim compensation. More recent state legislation mandates that local district attorneys' offices also distribute information about victim compensation.

Many states now recognize a wider range of economic losses. For instance, all states should follow Vermont's lead and change their policies to recognize ongoing crime-related expenses, and eliminate unnecessary filing deadlines. Three jurisdictions, Hawaii, Tennessee, and the Virgin Islands, provide compensation for non-economic losses. Even though their awards for pain and suffering are only a fraction of those provided by the September 11 Fund, they represent an acknowledgment that crime can exact both tangible and intangible costs. For victims who have experienced the cruelty of crime, and the deliberate nature of the pain inflicted on them, these awards can be quite meaningful. More states should consider the value of such a message.

In Vermont, Judy Rex, director of the Vermont Center for Crime Victim Services, which administers the state victim compensation program, has found ways to provide more generous assistance to victims. Rex introduced Parallel Justice principles as a strategic planning tool to make the Vermont program more victim-focused. Within only a few months, her agency implemented a profound shift in its approach to compensation. Previously, the agency, like most state compensation programs, would delineate what losses could and could not be reimbursed. After adopting a Parallel Justice approach, the agency now asks victims what they need, and then makes every effort to meet those needs. Thus the Vermont Center defined the correct priority—helping victims meet their needs, rather than limiting their access to compensation.

In addition, instead of requiring staff to review applications for proper documentation, leaving approval to the victim compensation board, staff now has authority to approve requests. The board reviews only those applications staff felt should be rejected, serving as a check on the exceptional decision to refuse a request for compensation. Now, according to Judy Rex, victims' requests for compensation for crime-related losses are almost always approved, and victims' needs are more likely to be met.

In the rare instances when victims in Vermont identify crime-related losses that seem inappropriate for compensation, staff tries to find other solutions. Several victims of domestic violence who continued to live in their homes after the batterers had been removed, applied for compensation to cover the cost of overdue utility payments, which previously had been covered by the batterers. The victims were at risk of losing services and earning bad credit ratings. Identifying these debts as a crime-related harm, the state compensation program entered into discussions with the state utilities agency to develop a debt-forgiveness program for these victims, similar to programs that already exist in other states (e.g., Indiana and Rhode Island). The Vermont efforts are particularly noteworthy because they were initiated by a government agency seeking to fulfill its commitment to help victims recover from crime-related losses, even when the specific losses were not covered by their mandate.

FORUMS AND OTHER OPPORTUNITIES TO BE HEARD

Victims are often asked to say what happened to them. Within the criminal justice context, when police first respond to a call for assistance, they want to know what happened. Later, investigators may want more details. Prosecutors may ask victims to testify at trial. They may submit a victim impact statement at sentencing. Victims may tell the story outside of the criminal justice process — to a doctor, a neighbor, or a member of the clergy.

These "listeners" are undeniably valuable to crime victims. But the

principles of Parallel Justice call for another type of listener: someone who is authorized to identify the full range of victims' needs, and
to develop a comprehensive response to those needs. Whether they
are called case managers, victim advocates, Parallel Justice specialists, or specially designated government officials, the listeners should
have the authority to mobilize local public and private resources, and
help victims access those resources in the most efficient way possible. Their mission is both to coordinate a just communal response
to an individual victim, and to strengthen the pathways to justice
for all victims.

A Parallel Justice case manager is not the same as a traditional
victim advocate. Successful victim advocates develop effective relationships with criminal justice and social service agency officials,
which enable them to access assistance that might not otherwise be
available. In these cases, it is the skillful negotiation of the advocate,
the compassion of the agency official, or even the timing of the victim's request that make the difference. Even the best victim advocate,
however, is relying on the power of persuasion to see that a victim's
rights are implemented, or that a victim receives needed services and
resources. By contrast, in a Parallel Justice framework, case managers who work with victims are part of a community-wide initiative.
When established by executive authority, and supported by the community and private sectors, a Parallel Justice initiative, and thus the
case managers working within it, has authority to marshal resources
on behalf of the victim.

Parallel Justice principles encourage us to create many opportunities for crime victims to explain what happened to them and to request
assistance. All government agencies in regular contact with victims,
particularly within the criminal justice, social service, and healthcare
systems, should create mechanisms to facilitate communication with
them. This function is best performed by in-house victim advocates,
but can also be handled by line staff trained to solicit feedback from
victims and encourage them to express their needs and concerns.

Jurisdictions should also create separate forums in which victims can describe the impact the crime has had on their lives, and explain what resources they need to get back on track. These forums can serve a number of important purposes. First, they can be vehicles for establishing accountability for the quality of services for victims. Specifically, they should provide opportunities for victims to lodge complaints about inadequate services, unreasonable policies, or systemic neglect by government agencies. The forum can also provide a hearing for victims to talk about issues that cut across government and nonprofit agencies.

Second, the forums can reinforce the principle that justice flows from a communal response. While that response occurs at different times and comes from many sectors of our society, victims need opportunities to tell their story to someone with government authority who represents this communal response. Unlike the criminal justice process, a forum established pursuant to Parallel Justice principles is created solely for victims and the process is focused on them. In contrast to a victim impact statement at sentencing, the forums provide victims an opportunity not only to review their experience of the crime and the impact on their lives, but also to explain what assistance they need to move forward.

An excellent example of a two-tiered forum has been established for the city of Burlington, Vermont, with two government-funded Parallel Justice specialists and a twenty-two-member Parallel Justice Commission, established through state and local executive orders. Commission members are appointed by the mayor of Burlington and the governor of Vermont. The commission is chaired by the head of a local nonprofit victim services organization, and comprised of high level officials including the mayor and the police chief, heads of several state and local government agencies, and leaders of nonprofit, community social service, and healthcare organizations. The Parallel Justice specialists are case managers, available to meet with victims of any kind of crime immediately after occurrence. One works alongside a victim advocate in the Police Department, the other is based in the local Community Justice Center. They provide supportive counseling, information about victims' rights, and assistance in accessing resources and services throughout Burlington. They also can tap the local resource bank, created by the Parallel Justice initiative, which provides emergency cash assistance and disperses donated items and services to crime victims.

When a victim's experience indicates that the communal response needs improvement, or that an agency's policies and protocols are problematic, the two Parallel Justice specialists can suggest that the situation be brought to the attention of the Parallel Justice Commission either through direct testimony by the victim, or a presentation by the Parallel Justice specialist. The commission, which meets on a quarterly basis, will then discuss cases such as these, which highlight a need to improve the community, criminal justice, or broader governmental response to victims. The Parallel Justice Commission has a duel mission: to address the needs of the individual victim in the case before them, and to eliminate interagency or systemic barriers highlighted by the victim's experience.

Box 4.1 **FORUM CASE STUDY**

The development of the Burlington Parallel Justice Commission illustrates the principle of a communal response to crime and the value of providing forums for victims. Recognizing that the commission was going to be engaged in ground-breaking work, all of the commission members participated in training to increase their understanding of the trauma and disruption experienced by many victims, enhance their ability to listen to victims in a nonjudgmental way, and learn how to solve problems more collaboratively. In addition each member was asked to examine the policies and practices of their own organization and work proactively to align them with Parallel Justice principles.

At its first few meetings, commission members learned more about Parallel Justice principles, and talked generally about ways to initiate internal reviews of their respective agencies. The commission was then ready to think collaboratively about inter-agency efforts to support Parallel Justice principles. At the commission's third meeting, a victim told the following story and encouraged the commission to take action.

One evening in September 2006, "Frank" was knocked unconscious a block from his house while walking home after dinner. A bystander helped him get home and then returned to the scene of the crime, where a fight was in progress. The police soon arrived and the bystander told them about Frank and gave them his address. A half dozen police officers came to Frank's house and, even though his brother was willing to take him to the hospital, insisted on calling an ambulance. As he was put on the gurney, Frank was given a breathalyzer test and photos were taken. At the hospital, he was treated and released. The defendants were given citations and told to appear in court for arraignment.

Frank learned about the Burlington Parallel Justice Project through outreach materials, and went to see the Parallel Justice specialist at the Burlington Community Justice Center. He identified several issues of concern. The crime turned his world upside down and made him feel guilty and unsafe. He felt unsupported by the criminal justice response. He objected to being given a breathalyzer test, particularly knowing the defendants were not given one. He complained that police officers showed up at his house unannounced four times, asking him to accompany them in the police car to point out the house the defendants came from before the assault. On the night of the crime, the investigating police officer gave him a specific date for an arraignment for early November, creating an expectation that he would get information about the case quickly. The case papers went back and forth between the police department and the State's Attorney's Office several times, postponing the arraignment first till January and then to May. It was over eight months before his experience became a "case" and he was contacted by the victim advocate in the State's Attorney's Office. When Frank finally received a letter from the State's Attorney's Office stating the disposition of the case, the language was hard to understand. The letter informed Frank that the defendants had received a sentence of community service, but he was never informed what service they performed. Frank felt strongly that the community service work should be meaningful.

In addition to his complaints about the criminal justice response, Frank was also unhappy with the treatment he received from the hospital. He felt that the hospital emergency room personnel did not respond thoroughly to the injuries he sustained. Frank was also quite concerned about his credit rating. He had received many telephone calls from a collection agency in the spring inquiring about unpaid hospital bills, even though Frank had been told that the victim compensation program would cover his medical bills.

The Parallel Justice specialist was able to give Frank a great deal of information nobody else had explained to him such as why the police wanted him to travel in an ambulance, the purpose of the breathalyzer test, and why arraignments are often postponed. The specialist was also able to smooth the way for compensation to cover Frank's medical expenses. It was clear however, that Frank's experience reflected a lack of communication and a lack of victim-oriented protocols, not only between officials and Frank, but also between various agencies. As a result, the Parallel Justice Project team, consisting of specialists, a supervisor, and the project coordinator, decided to bring the case to the full commission.

Frank was given the option of presenting his case himself or having the specialist present it on his behalf. He chose to speak directly to the commissioners, who saw immediately how much better the communal response to Frank could have been. The commission agreed to the following action steps, all to be completed before its next quarterly meeting: The State's Attorney's Office would review the letters sent to victims and clarify the language; the police department and the State's Attorney's Office would review the procedures involved in preparing a case for prosecution to minimize the time between arrest and arraignment; the police department would create a protocol requiring officers to explain police procedures to victims when asking them to take a breathalyzer test or ride in an ambulance; the Vermont Center for Crime Victim Services, which oversees victim compensation in Vermont and the hospital would design a protocol to ensure that victims' bills are not sent to collection agencies when they will be covered by compensation; and finally, the hospital would train emergency room personnel in Parallel Justice principles to ensure that victims receive information about Parallel Justice and other victim service resources, and that victims are treated with more sensitivity and respect.

According to Sharon Davis, special projects coordinator for the Vermont Center for Crime Victim Services, the feeling in the room after this meeting was that "responsibility for addressing crime victims' needs in Burlington had evolved into a broader community-wide obligation and Parallel Justice had taken hold."

Communities should design these "opportunities to be heard" taking into account the local culture of decision-making and interagency collaboration. Whether a forum provides an opportunity for a victim to speak with a few high-level officials or a panel of representatives from several different agencies, the forums need to be dynamic mechanisms with the authority to marshal resources on behalf of individual victims, address gaps in services, and overcome systemic barriers to providing Parallel Justice to victims of crime.

All participants in these forums must be trained to listen carefully and to demonstrate respect and compassion for the victims before them. They must learn how to ask questions that illuminate victims' circumstances without blaming them for the crime. Whatever design a community chooses for the forums, the ongoing communal response to a particular victim should be coordinated by a case manager authorized to marshal government and community-based resources on behalf of the victim. Forums should be linked to this case management function so that the needs identified by crime victims are addressed efficiently through a coordinated response.

How Can We Pay for All This?

Implementing Parallel Justice requires more than our collective will, it requires a commitment of public funds. Some of these funds, though, are already committed in the budgets of social service agencies, so embracing Parallel Justice principles would simply require that victims of crime be given a priority in the allocation of those funds.

For example, crime victims may need new housing in order to relocate, or may require substance-abuse treatment, job training, or emergency daycare as they forge new lives. Many communities provide some or all of these services, and victims may already be eligible to receive them. To reach these victims, however, these services need to be viewed as more than a response to homelessness, substance abuse, or unemployment. They should be considered critical ingredients in providing justice to victims of crime. Whenever possible, crime victims' experiences should be factored into decisions about triaging services, and their crime-related needs should be considered high priorities.

Many of the Parallel Justice-oriented policies and practices described in this chapter will not require additional public funding. For example, it doesn't cost anything for government officials or social service and healthcare providers to treat victims with respect and acknowledge that what happened to them was wrong. Similarly, to focus on preventing repeat victimization or to redeploy private sector and community-based services to assist victims need not entail new resources. But it is important to realize that simply reallocating funds will not be sufficient to support Parallel Justice initiatives. Additional public funds will be required to meet society's obligation to crime victims.

Our state and federal governments currently spend billions of dollars each year in response to crime. At the federal level, under the 1994 Violent Crime Control and Law Enforcement Act alone, Congress appropriated over $5 billion to hire new police officers, and over $2 billion for state prison construction.[33] According to the Bureau of Justice Statistics, state and federal government combined spent $214 billion in 2006 on the operations of the criminal justice system.[34]

The federal government also allocates funds for crime victims, but far less than for other criminal justice purposes. Under the Victims of Crime Act, the federal government gives states approximately $500,000 each year for victim assistance.[35] It is noteworthy that all of this money comes from fines and penalties paid by offenders in the federal criminal justice system—none of it is appropriated from general tax revenues. There is something fundamentally wrong with committing federal tax dollars to fund every aspect of our nation's response to crime except helping victims rebuild their lives.[36] While people who commit crime should contribute to the effort, providing justice to victims should be viewed as a communal responsibility, one we all share. Forging a national commitment to help all victims of any kind of crime requires committing tax dollars to the effort, not just relying on offender fines to accomplish the task.

The costs of implementing the Parallel Justice ideas discussed in this chapter will vary depending on the level of preexisting resources and the magnitude of victims' needs in any given community. Some of the Parallel Justice initiatives already underway across the country have been funded by private foundations or businesses, others by state and federal government grants, and still others are underway without any additional funding. Each of the communities trying to achieve Parallel Justice has found creative ways to tap a range of resources to support this work.

It is clear, however, that because of our nation's failure to dedicate sufficient resources to help victims of crime, our society has incurred enormous costs. Although these costs have been borne by society at large, we know they are concentrated in communities where crime is highest, and thus are felt particularly acutely in poor communities of color.

Every year millions of Americans become crime victims. Many change their lives dramatically. Some stay home at night. Others restrict themselves to certain neighborhoods. Some abuse drugs or alcohol to cope with their pain. Some become anxious, depressed, or suicidal. Others lose their jobs because they have crime-related disabilities or because they missed work to attend court. Some become so alienated from others that they withdraw from community life. Some victims learn violent behavior and eventually become criminals themselves.

All of these outcomes constitute enormous losses to society. Thus, an increased investment of funds to address the needs of crime victims should return enormous benefits in reduced trauma, increased social interactions, sustained productivity, enhanced quality of life, and safer communities. One of the most important benefits—but the one most difficult to measure in financial terms—should be a greater appreciation by victims that justice has been served.

This portrait of Parallel Justice on the ground is a snapshot of only some of the actions that can be taken informed by the guiding principles of Parallel Justice. Every agency of the criminal justice system—police, prosecutors, courts, and corrections—is called upon to make a series of changes in its basic operations to respond differently to victims' needs. Every social service and healthcare agency could reorient its core business practices to help victims. Every sector of our civil society—businesses, employers, schools, neighbors and faith-based institutions—can make a contribution to Parallel Justice. At the most fundamental level, these actions reflect a new vision of justice for victims of crime. The only remaining question is how to get started implementing this new vision, a question addressed in the next chapter.

5

Getting Started

Parallel Justice is a big idea requiring significant transformation of our response to victims of crime. But operationalizing the Parallel Justice framework need not be daunting. Parallel Justice is not a blueprint that prescribes a specific set of policies and practices; rather, it's a concept based on principles that can guide a communal response to victims. Once a critical mass of people in a community decides to implement Parallel Justice initiatives, there are many ways to get started. This final chapter sets forth six guidelines to translate those principles into a plan to convert Parallel Justice from an idea to a reality.

1 Build A Strong Foundation of Public Understanding

To be successful, a Parallel Justice initiative must be firmly rooted in a deep public understanding of the needs of crime victims. One of the best ways to spark interest in Parallel Justice is to create greater public awareness about the impact of crime, the inadequacy of our current response, and the terrible price society pays as a result. Few people know how limited the resources available to victims are, and how damaging it is to both individuals and society when victims do not get the help they need. Explaining the connections between victimization and drug abuse and alcoholism, depression and suicide, teen pregnancy, poor academic and job performance, repeat victimization, and, for many, lives leading to criminal behavior, is key to recruiting support from people outside the traditional victim services field.

To get started, it can be very effective for a community leader to articulate these truths. In Redlands, California, the chief of police kicked off that community's Parallel Justice efforts. Realizing that most people's understanding of victimization was limited to brief media accounts of particular crimes, he spoke about the long-term impact of crime on individuals and communities. By taking advantage of his many opportunities to address the public, he made the connection between victimization and healthcare costs, low productivity, and many of the social ills that plague communities. Soon, local businesses wanted to participate in the Parallel Justice initiative because they understood that helping victims was not only good for victims but also good for the local economy.

The example from Redlands underscores the importance of building support for Parallel Justice, rooted in an understanding of the issues confronting crime victims. The advocate for this viewpoint need not be the chief of police, of course, but the effort is best led by a respected organization or individual who can mobilize public support and is committed to a sustained effort over a long period of time.

2 CREATE BROAD-BASED SUPPORT FOR REFORM

Fostering the public will to take action is essential to implementing this new vision of justice for crime victims, and requires bringing together a cross-section of private, community-based, and government agencies to develop a comprehensive local plan of action.

Both the private and public sectors must be engaged, but the effort can begin almost anywhere. Over the last few years, several communities have developed Parallel Justice initiatives through the creative efforts of different types of leaders. In North Carolina, for example, the effort was led by a university-based research organization focusing primarily on community safety and prisoner reentry. In California, police officials endorsed the idea first, and launched a public-awareness campaign. In Vermont, corrections officials created the initial momentum, and now the Vermont Center for Crime Victim Services (an agency of state government), the Burlington Police Department, and the Burlington Community and Economic Development Office jointly administer the Parallel Justice effort.

Each of these leaders established multidisciplinary, broad-based task forces to design and implement Parallel Justice initiatives, building on local resources to address local crime victims' needs. These task forces should include victims, victim advocates, representatives from all the criminal justice agencies, the healthcare and social service systems, community development organizations, the business and the faith communities, and local government officials and elected leaders. Decision-makers should be invited to the table.

Early on, proponents of Parallel Justice should engage the press and local philanthropic organizations as well, so they can join efforts to educate the public and build more support for the initiative. For example, in Winston-Salem, North Carolina, the Parallel Justice task force convened meetings with journalists and foundation leaders to demonstrate the connection between victimization and the impact on the local community. The team, led by a former journalist, made a concerted effort to change the conversation about crime from one exclusively focused on individual cases to a broader analysis of the cost of crime on individuals, families, and the community at large. Soon, local media began to produce feature articles about the impact of crime on communities, and prominent local foundations began discussions about creating a local resource bank for victims.

3 BASE THE ARGUMENT FOR REFORM ON SOLID RESEARCH

Parallel Justice initiatives should be informed by data on local crime and victimization trends, victims' needs, and service capacity. The most accurate — albeit labor-intensive — way to gather the victim-oriented information is to conduct a random household victimization survey to measure the nature and prevalence of victimization. The U.S. Department of Justice annually sponsors such a survey, the National Crime Victimization Survey (NCVS), which is available from the Bureau of Justice Statistics. Local communities can tailor the survey instrument to assess local needs, by adding questions about the immediate and long-term impact of crime, as well as what assistance victims needed and what they received. Structured in this way, victimization surveys reveal far more about the emotional, physical, and financial consequences of crime than police reports do. Implementing a local crime victimization survey, as a number of jurisdictions have done, provides a solid launch pad for a Parallel Justice initiative.

Focus groups with victims and staff of victim services agencies are another way to learn about victims' needs and local service capacity. Depending on local resources, the Parallel Justice task force can also convene groups organized by type of crime and/or characteristics of the victims (age, gender, race, etc.) to elicit more specific information. For example, the state of Maryland was interested in learning more about the experience of crime victims — the effectiveness of official responses, and the shortfall in victim services — and commissioned the National Center for Victims of Crime to conduct a series of focus groups with victims and service providers.[1] In the state of New York, the Downstate Victims Coalition, as part of its early Parallel Justice work, decided to survey victim advocates at a state conference to gain a more detailed understanding of how well victims' needs were being met.

Whatever method of gathering information is used, it should include opportunities for victims to speak openly about how crime has changed their lives and what kind of responses, resources or services would have been helpful. For example, in preparation for the Parallel Justice Project in Burlington, the Vermont Center for Crime Victim Services convened several focus groups to understand how crime affected local residents. In addition to learning if social services and criminal justice agencies met the needs and expectations of victims, the organizers asked victims open-ended questions about what would have helped them move on with their lives. One woman told how she had been sexually assaulted when she had been out jogging, and was too afraid to resume her passion of running. What she wanted most was someone she could trust who would run with her. Months later, as the Parallel Justice task force solicited donations for the newly established victims' resource bank, a local sports shop invited victims to join their runners' group, or if they preferred, the shop would provide running partners. By asking open-ended questions, the task force obtained information that led to the availability of a nontraditional response, one that may be even more important to some victims than typical victim services.

Parallel Justice initiatives must also be evaluated for their effectiveness in keeping victims safe and creating a sense that justice has been served. Process and impact evaluations can help communities determine how well Parallel Justice principles have been implemented, the degree to which various sectors of the community have become involved, the perceptions of victims regarding their treatment, and how their lives were changed in the immediate aftermath of crime as a result of Parallel Justice responses. Longitudinal research will lead to greater understanding about the long-term impact of Parallel Justice responses, whether they are effective in reducing many of the social ills that often accompany victimization, and whether they lower the cost of crime for both individual victims and for communities.

4 INVENTORY THE CURRENT RESPONSE TO VICTIMS

Developing a menu of services currently in place to meet the needs of local victims will establish a baseline from which to grow the Parallel Justice initiative. Communities that have any victim services at all typically offer prosecution-based victim/witness assistance for those victims whose cases have made it to the prosecution stage of the justice process. Many also offer rape crisis counseling and services for battered women. Few are currently able to provide sufficient resources for these victims, or any assistance at all for victims of other kinds of crime. Once a baseline has been established, the local Parallel Justice task force should analyze the shortfall between existing resources and the assistance that should be available. The task force should also review the various stages of the community's interaction with victims and document whether each stage is or is not aligned with Parallel Justice principles.

The task force should first determine whether the jurisdiction's immediate response to victims is adequate. For example, does it address their need for safety and prevention of repeat victimization? Does it include information, crisis counseling, and practical help such as emergency financial assistance, trauma-informed healthcare, crime scene cleanup, and replacing broken locks or windows? Then the team should look at what kind of ongoing assistance is provided such as counseling, safety planning, healthcare, housing, daycare, transportation, and employment support. In many communities it would also be useful to inventory neighborhood groups, civic associations, and faith-based institutions. They may be called upon to join the Parallel Justice initiative, even if they are currently not directly involved in victim assistance. Finally, the team should examine the policies and practices of all government agencies that interact with victims, as well as the status of victims' rights within the jurisdiction.

Such an inventory focuses discussions about how best to structure a Parallel Justice initiative, taking into account current laws and the network of preexisting victim services, as well as other criminal justice, social service, or healthcare agencies, community organizations, and businesses. By using the Parallel Justice principles as a yardstick to evaluate state laws and the organizational capabilities of local agencies, the task force begins to develop a substantive agenda for serious reform.

5 DEVELOP PARALLEL JUSTICE PRIORITIES

Once organizers have created a multidisciplinary Parallel Justice task force, gathered information about local crime and victimization, documented the gaps in services and resources available to victims, and identified untapped community resources, the task force can begin to determine priorities for a local initiative.

For example, task forces making victim safety a top priority could think creatively with police and other criminal justice officials about how to redeploy existing resources with a greater emphasis on victim safety through each phase of the criminal justice process from the initial police response and investigation through prosecution, sentencing, and release from prison. The task force could also think about the most important ways local schools, businesses, hospitals, and other institutions could change their policies and practices to keep victims safer, whether or not an offender is ever apprehended.

This analysis is akin to the kinds of audits that have been conducted of social services and healthcare systems to see if they reflect new knowledge about a topic. For example, Vermont has analyzed how services delivered by the state could be changed to reflect the latest knowledge about the impact of trauma on individuals. In other words, they have asked what "trauma-informed" systems would do differently and what would it take to make those changes. Similarly, all local criminal justice agencies, schools, hospitals, and other institutions could review their operations to see which policies and practices should be changed to reflect a greater emphasis on victim safety.

Similar questions could be asked about each of the Parallel Justice principles:

- ► What would it take to presume that all victims are credible unless there is reason to believe otherwise?

- ► What policies and practices need to be changed so that victims experience no further harm?

- ► What opportunities can be created for victims to explain what happened to them, and articulate what they need to regain control over their lives?

- ► How does the community communicate that what happened to victims was wrong, and that every effort will be made to help them rebuild their lives?

Instead of focusing on one principle at a time, an alternative approach would be to select agencies or organizations, and develop strategies to infuse all Parallel Justice principles throughout their operations. A local team might decide to focus first on one or more criminal justice agencies, social service providers, the local health-care system, or even the business sector. Alternatively, the team might decide to begin with a legislative analysis to determine the shortfalls in a state's laws and then develop a legislative agenda based on Parallel Justice principles. These decisions should be guided by local needs, resources, and interests.

Whichever strategy is chosen, however, while the team is working on grander reforms, it should look for ways to demonstrate the value of Parallel Justice with actions that are easily accomplished and will have a big impact. Seemingly small gestures (e.g., adding new language to a probation officer's letter to a victim—"What happened to you is wrong and I'll do all I can to assist you") have enormous significance for victims and clearly demonstrate the relevance of the Parallel Justice framework.

6 CREATE A COMMUNICATIONS STRATEGY

A communications strategy can create both grassroots and institutional allies in efforts to achieve Parallel Justice. Once the task force is in place and has developed an initial plan of action, it can garner public support with a strong public education component. Community forums or workshops can introduce the concept of Parallel Justice, discuss the negative experiences of local crime victims, and show how things might have been handled differently under Parallel Justice.

The task force can brief the press about Parallel Justice, write op-ed pieces for local newspapers, create pamphlets, posters, and radio and TV public service announcements—essentially explore all local media opportunities for ways to expose the community to the concept of Parallel Justice. Web sites dealing with criminal justice and victim services should include links to Parallel Justice information. Government officials and other opinion leaders can use these resources to champion Parallel Justice in their speeches, their writing, and during meetings with the press.

In Burlington, Vermont, after the Parallel Justice initiative was officially launched, television, radio, and print public service announcements ran for several months highlighting a new way of responding to crime victims through "Justice, Burlington style." Posters and brochures were developed in seven languages. Special outreach efforts were made to the large student population, and the *Front Porch Forum,* an online community newsletter, helped spread the word. The multimedia campaign not only gave residents, business leaders, and government officials a new vocabulary, it also created a buzz about Parallel Justice and a sense that something better was possible for victims.

GETTING STARTED

The most important part of getting started is getting started. Parallel Justice will not look the same everywhere. Each community will develop different mechanisms for victims to be heard, to seek assistance, or complain about the treatment they have received. Each community will create different roles for local governments, and community-based organizations. Local businesses, civic associations, and faith institutions will have varying contributions to make. States will enact different legislation to address different statewide issues.

The commonalities however, will be apparent in all communities that adopt a Parallel Justice approach. Local designs will be informed by local data. Criminal justice agencies, as well as other government and community organizations, will be reoriented to keep the safety of victims in focus at all times. Regardless of whether their cases result in the arrest and prosecution of an offender, victims of any kind of crime will be offered immediate support, compensation for their losses, practical assistance, and an opportunity to be heard. Additional resources and services will be coordinated by case managers. Enforcing victims' legal rights will be a priority, and it will be clear that seeking justice for victims is not the responsibility of victim advocates alone. Parallel Justice will be viewed as a critical part of a community-wide response to crime.

Over the past generation, our society has made significant progress in developing a more compassionate response to victims of crime. We have also created new and important legal rights for victims. But we have not recognized our societal obligation to help victims of crime rebuild their lives.

Parallel Justice redefines what it means to serve the interests of justice. It affirms that a just society seeks not only to hold offenders accountable and, whenever possible, to reintegrate them into society, but also to keep victims safe and reintegrate them into productive communal life. We must meet our obligation to victims, not just because we are a compassionate society but because helping victims rebuild their lives is an essential component of justice.

⊣ | | | ⊢

RESOURCES

For assistance in developing Parallel Justice in your community, contact:

The Parallel Justice Project
www.paralleljustice.org

For resources and advocacy for crime victims and those who serve them, contact:

The National Center for Victims of Crime
www.ncvc.org

Notes

INTRODUCTION

1. Graham Farrell and Ken Pease, *Once Bitten, Twice Bitten: Repeat Victimization and its Implications for Crime Prevention,* Crime Prevention Unit Series Paper No. 46 (London, UK: Home Office Police Research Group, 1993).
2. Cathy Spatz Widom and Michael G. Maxfield, *An Update On The "Cycle of Violence,"* (Washington, DC: Department of Justice, Office of Justice Programs, National Institute of Justice 2001), 2.
3. Madeline Wordes and Michell Nunez, *Our Vulnerable Teenagers: Their Victimization, Its Consequences, and Directions for Prevention and Intervention* (Washington, DC: National Center for Victims of Crime, 2002), 14–15.

CHAPTER 1

1. R. Barry Ruback and Martie P. Thompson, *Social and Psychological Consequences of Violent Victimization* (Thousand Oaks, CA: Sage Publications, 2001), 87–105.
2. Michael Rand, *Criminal Victimization, 2007* (Washington, DC: Department of Justice, Office of Justice Programs, Bureau of Justice Statistics, 2008), 1.
3. Ibid., 2–7.
4. Department of Justice, Federal Bureau of Investigation, Criminal Justice Information Services Division, "Crime in the United States by Volume and Rate Per 100,000 Inhabitants 1988–2007," *Crime in the United*

States 2007, www.fbi.gov/ucr/cius2007/data/table_01.html.

5. James Q. Wilson, "Crime and Public Policy," in *Crime: Public Policies for Crime Control*, eds. James Q. Wilson and Joan Petersilia (Oakland, CA: Institute for Contemporary Studies, 2002), 540-1.

6. Rand, *Criminal Victimization, 2007*, 1.

7. Synovate, *Federal Trade Commission-2006 Identity Theft Survey Report* (Washington, D.C.: Federal Trade Commission, 2007), 3.

8. Katrina Baum, *Identity Theft, 2005* (Washington, DC: Department of Justice, Office of Justice Programs, Bureau of Justice Statistics, 2007), 1.

9. Rand, *Criminal Victimization, 2007*, 4.

10. Patsy Klaus, *Crimes Against Persons Age 65 or Older, 1993–2002* (Washington, DC: Department of Justice, Office of Justice Programs, Bureau of Justice Statistics, 2005), 1–2.

11. Rand, *Criminal Victimization, 2007*, 4.

12. David Finkelhor and Jennifer Dziuba-Leatherman, "Children as Victims of Violence: A National Survey," *Pediatrics* 94, no. 4 (1994): 413-20.

13. Rand, *Criminal Victimization, 2007*, 4.

14. Steven W. Perry, *American Indians and Crime* (Washington, DC: Department of Justice, Office of Justice Programs, Bureau of Justice Statistics, 2004), 4–8.

15. Department of Justice, Federal Bureau of Investigation, "Expanded Homicide Data Table 2-Murder Victims by Age, Sex, and Race 2007," *Crime in the United States, 2007* www.fbi.gov/ucr/cius07/offenses/expanded_information/data/shrtable_02.html.

16. *Black Homicide Victimization in the United States: An Analysis of 2006 Homicide Data* (Washington, DC: Violence Policy Center, 2009), 2.

17. Ibid., 2.

18. Centers for Disease Control and Prevention, National Center for Injury Prevention and Control, Office of Statistics and Programming, "10 Leading Causes of Death, United States, 2006, Black, Both Sexes," http://webappa.cdc.gov/sasweb/ncipc/leadcaus10.html.

19. L. Taylor and others, "Witnessing Violence By Young Children and Their Mothers," *Journal of Developmental and Behavioral Pediatrics* 15, no. 2 (1994): 120–123.

20. Kevin M. Fitzpatrick and Janet P. Boldizar, "The Prevalence and Consequences of Exposure to Violence Among African-American Youth," *Journal of the American Academy of Child and Adolescent Psychiatry* 32 (1993): 424–30.

21. Rand, *Criminal Victimization, 2007*, 5.

22. Jeremy Travis, *But They All Come Back: Facing the Challenges of Prisoner Reentry* (Washington, DC: The Urban Institute Press, 2005), 282.

23. David Kennedy, *Deterrence and Crime Prevention* (New York: Routledge, 2009), 42–5.

24. Rand, *Criminal Victimization, 2007*, 6.

25. Ibid, 7.

26. Timothy C. Hart and Callie Rennison, *Reporting Crime to the Police, 1992–2000* (Washington, DC: Department of Justice, Office of Justice Programs, Bureau of Justice Statistics, 2003), 7.

27. "Victim Satisfaction With the Criminal Justice System," *National Institute of Justice Journal*, no. 253 (2006), www.ojp.usdoj.gov/nij/journals/253/victim.html

28. Ibid.

29. National Center for Victims of Crime and the Police Foundation, *Bringing Victims Into Community Policing* (Washington, DC: Department of Justice, Office of Community Oriented Policing Services, 2002).

30. Graham Farrell and Adam C. Bouloukos, "International Overview: A Cross-National Comparison of Rates of Repeat Victimization," in *Repeat Victimization: Crime Prevention Studies*, Vol. 12, eds. Graham Farrell and Ken Pease (Monsey, NY: Criminal Justice Press, 2001), 7–11.

31. Ibid., 11.

32. Graham Farrell and Ken Pease, *Once Bitten, Twice Bitten: Repeat Victimization and its Implications for Crime Prevention*, Crime Prevention Unit Series Paper No. 46 (London, UK: Home Office Police Research Group, 1993), 7.

33. Deborah Lamm Weisel, *Analyzing Repeat Victimization, Problem-Oriented Guides For Police-Problem Solving Tools* Series No. 4 (Washington, DC: Department of Justice, Office of Community Oriented Policing Services, 2005), 9.

34. Ibid., 11.

35. Dan Ellingworth, Graham Farrell, and Ken Pease, "A Victim Is A Victim Is A Victim? Chronic Victimization in Four Sweeps of the British Crime Survey," *British Journal of Criminology* 35, no. 3 (1995): 363.

36. Edward R. Kleemans, "Repeat Burglary Victimization: Results of Empirical Research in the Netherlands," in *Repeat Victimization, Crime Prevention Studies* Volume 12, ed. Graham Farrell and Ken Pease (Monsey, NY: Criminal Justice Press, 2001), 58.

37. Weisel, *Analyzing Repeat Victimization*, 7.

38. Frank Morgan, "Repeat Burglary in a Perth Suburb," in *Repeat Victimization, Crime Prevention Studies* Volume 12, ed. Graham Farrell and Ken Pease (Monsey, NY: Criminal Justice Press, 2001), 87.

39. Dean G. Kilpatrick and Ron Acierno, "Mental Health Needs of Crime Victims: Epidemiology and Outcomes," *Journal of Traumatic Stress* 16, no. 2 (2003): 124.

40. Catalina M. Arata, "Child Sexual Abuse and Sexual Revictimization," *Clinical Psychology: Science and Practice* 9, no. 2 (2002): 135.

41. Leah E. Daigle, Bonnie S. Fisher, and Pamela Guthrie, "The Reoccurrence of Victimization," in *Victims of Crime*, 3rd ed., eds. Robert C. Davis, Arthur J. Lurigio and Susan Herman (Thousand Oaks, CA: Sage Publications, 2007), 217.

42. Jalna Hanmer and Elizabeth Stanko, "Stripping Away the Rhetoric of Protection: Violence to Women, Law and the State in Britain and the USA," *International Journal of the Sociology of Law* 13 (1985): 366.

43. Sam Lloyd, Graham Farrell and Ken Pease, *Preventing Repeated Domestic Violence: A Demonstration Project on Merseyside,* Crime Prevention Unit Series Paper No. 49 (London, UK: Home Office Police Department, 1994), 2.

44. Ibid., 3.

45. Weisel, *Analyzing Repeat Victimization*, 12–14.

46. Judith Lewis Herman, *Trauma and Recovery* (New York: Basic Books, 1992), 34.

47. Marlene A. Young, *Meeting Victim Needs: What Is the Role of Victim Compensation In Recovery?* (Washington, DC: National Center for Victims of Crime, 2003), 6.

48. Kilpatrick and Acierno, "Mental Health Needs of Crime Victims," 130.

49. "Anxiety Disorders: Traumatic Stress Disorders," in *DSM-IV-TR Mental Disorders: Diagnosis, Etiology, and Treatment,* eds. Michael B. First and Allan Tasman (West Sussex, UK: John Wiley & Sons, Ltd., 2004), 927–8.

50. Kilpatrick and Acierno, "Mental Health Needs of Crime Victims," 126.

51. "The Fundamentals of Mental Health and Mental Illness," in *Mental Health: A Report of the Surgeon General* (Rockville, MD: Department of Health and Human Services, U.S. Public Health Service, 1999), table 2.6.

52. Rochelle F. Hanson and others, "Violent Crime and Mental Health," in *Traumatic Stress: From Theory to Practice,* Plenum Series On Stress and Coping, eds. John R. Freedy and Stevan E. Hobfoll (New York: Springer, 1995), 145.

53. Dean G. Kilpatrick, *The Mental Health Impact of Rape,* National Violence Against Women Prevention Research Center, www.vawprevention.org/research/mentalimpact.shtml.

54. "The Fundamentals of Mental Health and Mental Illness," table 2.6.

55. Evan Stark and Anne Flitcraft, *Women at Risk: Domestic Violence and Women's Health* (Thousand Oaks, CA: Sage Publications, 1996), 162–163.

56. Carey Conley Thomson, et al., "Caretaker-Child Concordance for Child's Exposure to Violence in a Preadolescent Inner-City Population," *Archives of Pediatrics & Adolescent Medicine* 156, no. 8 (2002): 818–23.

57. Jay G. Silverman, et al., "Dating Violence Against Adolescent Girls and Associated Substance Use, Unhealthy Weight Control, Sexual Risk Behavior, Pregnancy, and Suicidality," *Journal of the American Medical Association* 286, no. 5 (2001): 574–5.

58. Kilpatrick and Acierno "Mental Health Needs of Crime Victims," 124–5.

59. Madeline Wordes and Michelle Nunez, *Our Vulnerable Teenagers: Their Victimization, Its Consequences, and Directions for Prevention and Intervention* (Washington, DC: National Center for Victims of Crime, 2002), 14–5.

60. Jennifer N. Shaffer and R. Barry Ruback, *Violent Victimization as a Risk Factor for Violent Offending Among Juveniles* (Washington, DC: Department of Justice, Office of Justice Programs, Office of Juvenile Delinquency Prevention, 2002), 6–7.

61. Cathy Spatz Widom, "The Cycle of Violence," *Science* 244, no. 4901 (1989): 164.

62. Debbie Deem, Lisa Nerenberg, and Richard Titus, "Victims of Financial Crime," in *Victims of Crime,* 3rd ed., eds. Robert C. Davis, Arthur J. Lurigio and Susan Herman (Thousand Oaks, CA: Sage Publications, 2007), 133.

63. Ibid.

64. Ibid., 134.

65. PTSD results from the inability to stop replaying a particularly horrific, traumatic event or events. While financial crime can be devastating, it has not been associated with this particular reaction.

66. Linda Ganzini, Benston McFarland, and Joseph Bloom, "Victims of Fraud: Comparing Victims of While Collar and Violent Crime," *Bulletin of the American Academy of Psychiatry and the Law* 18, no. 1 (1990): 55–63.

67. Robert J. Sampson, "The Community," in *Crime: Public Policies for Crime Control,* eds. James Q. Wilson and Joan Petersilia (Oakland, CA: Institute for Contemporary Studies, 2002), 237–40.

68. Laura Dugan, "The Effect of Criminal Victimization on a Household's Moving Decision," *Criminology* 37, no. 4 (1999): 913.

69. Sampson, "The Community," 237–40.

70. Ibid.

71. Deborah Bybee and Cris M. Sullivan, "Predicting Re-Victimization of Battered Women 3 Years After Exiting a Shelter Program," *American Journal of Community Psychology* 36, nos. 1, 2 (2005): 86–7.

72. *Criminal Victimization In The United States,* 2005 Statistical Tables (Washington, DC: Department of Justice, Office of Justice Programs, Bureau of Justice Statistics, 2006), 98.

73. Ibid., 96.

74. Deem, "Victims of Financial Crime," 133.

75. *Costs of Intimate Partner Violence against Women in the United States* (Atlanta, GA: Department of Health and Human Services, Centers For Disease Control and Prevention, National Center for Injury Prevention and Control, 2003), 25–6.

76. Synovate, *Federal Trade Commission–Identity Theft Survey Report* (Washington, D.C.: Federal Trade Commission, 2003), 6.

77. Synovate, *Federal Trade Commission–2006 Identity Theft Survey Report,* 4–9.

78. Ted R. Miller, Mark A. Cohen, and Brian Wiersema, *Victim Costs and Consequences: A New Look* (Washington, DC: Department of Justice, National Institute of Justice, 1996), 1.

79. Ibid.

80. *Costs of Intimate Partner Violence against Women in the United States,* 2.

81. Miller, *Victim Costs and Consequences,* 9.

CHAPTER 2

1. *New Directions for the Field: Victims' Rights and Services for the 21st Century* (Washington, DC: Department of Justice, Office of Justice Programs, Office for Victims of Crime, 1998), 325.

2. Susan Herman and Michelle Waul, *Repairing the Harm: A New Vision for Crime Victim Compensation in America* (Washington, DC: National Center for Victims of Crime, 2004), 19.

3. Department of Justice, Office of Justice Programs, Office for Victims of Crime, "1998 Victims of Crime Act of 1984 Performance Report State Compensation Program," *Nationwide Analysis-Victims of Crime Act,* www.ojp.usdoj.gov/ovc/fund/vocanpr_vc98_1.html.

4. Department of Justice, Office of Justice Programs, Office for Victims of Crime, "2008 Victims of Crime Act of 1984 Performance Report State Compensation Program," *Nationwide Analysis-Victims of Crime Act,* www.ojp.usdoj.gov/ovc/fund/vocanpr_vc08.html.

5. Department of Justice, Office for Victims of Crime, Office of Justice Programs, "Victims of Crime Act Victim Compensation Grant Program," *Federal Registrar* 66, no. 95 (2001): 27158–61.

6. Herman and Waul, *Repairing the Harm,* 30–1.

7. Ibid., 30.

8. Lisa Newmark et al., *The National Evaluation of State Victims of Crime Act Assistance and Compensation Programs: Trends and Strategies for the Future* (Washington, D.C.: Urban Institute, 2003), 109.

9. U.S. Code: Title 42, Chapter 112, Section 10602: *Crime Victim Compensation* (42 USC 10602).

10. Herman and Waul, *Repairing the Harm,* 23.

11. Michael Rand, *Criminal Victimization, 2007* (Washington, DC: Department of Justice, Office of Justice Programs, Bureau of Justice Statistics, 2008), 4.

12. David Finkelhor and others, "Victimization of Children and Youth: A Comprehensive National Survey," *Child Maltreatment* 10, no. 1 (2005), 5.

13. Cathy Spatz Widom and Michael G. Maxfield, *An Update On the "Cycle of Violence,"* (Washington, DC: Department of Justice, Office of Justice Programs, National Institute of Justice 2001), 5.

14. Rand, *Criminal Victimization, 2007,* 1.

15. Debbie Deem, Lisa Nerenberg, and Richard Titus, "Victims of Financial Crime," in *Victims of Crime,* 3rd ed., ed. Robert C. Davis, Arthur J. Lurigio and Susan Herman (Thousand Oaks, CA: Sage Publications, 2007), 136.

16. Lisa Newmark, *Crime Victims' Needs and VOCA-Funded Services: Findings and Recommendations from Two National Studies* (Alexandria, VA: Institute for Law and Justice, 2004), 20–21.

17. The Web site of the Office of Victims of Crime of the US Department of Justice includes a national directory of victim services offered by a wide range of agencies from traditional victim service providers to hospitals, social service agencies, and faith-based organizations. There are twenty-four categories of services listed for those agencies. None of them focus on preventing repeat victimization for all victims of crime. The closest category listed is safety planning, which in this context is limited to creating plans to prevent continued stalking.

18. Melissa Labriola, Michael Rampel, and Robert C. Davis, *Testing the Effectiveness of Batterer Programs and Judicial Monitoring* (New York: Center for Court Innovation, 2005), viii.

19. Edward W. Gondolf, "The Effect of Batterer Counseling on Shelter Outcome," *Journal of Interpersonal Violence* 3, no. 3 (1988): 285–6.

20. Patrick A. Langan and David P. Farrington, *Crime and Justice in the United States and in England and Wales, 1981–96* (Washington, DC: Department of Justice Programs, Bureau of Justice Statistics, 1998), 19.

21. Robert C. Davis, "Victim/Witness Noncooperation: A Second Look at a Persistent Phenomenon," *Journal of Criminal Justice* 11, no. 4 (1983): 293.

22. Council of State Governments Eastern Regional Conference, *What Do We Want (and What Are We Getting) From The Criminal Justice System?* (New York: Council of State Governments, 1999), 6.

23. "Victim Satisfaction with the Criminal Justice System," *National Institute of Justice Journal,* no. 253 (2006): par. 1, www.ojp.usdoj.gov/nij/journals/253/victim.html.

24. Andrew Karmen, *Crime Victims: An Introduction to Victimology,* 4th ed. (Belmont, CA: Wadsworth Thomson Learning, 2001), 140.

25. *Criminal Victimization in the United States 1973* (Washington, DC: Department of Justice, Law Enforcement Assistance Administration, National Criminal Justice Information and Statistics Service, 1976), 58.

26. Davis, "Victim/Witness Noncooperation," 288.

27. Robert C. Davis, *Impact Evaluation of the Victim/Witness Assistance Project's Appearance Management Activities* (New York: Vera Institute of Justice, 1976), 1–3.

28. Robert C. Davis, "Mediation: The Brooklyn Experiment," in *Neighborhood Justice: Assessment of an Emerging Idea,* eds. R. Tomasic and M.M. Feeley (New York: Longman, 1982), 162.

29. Robert C. Davis, Frances Kunreuther, and Elizabeth Connick, "Expanding the Victim's Role in the Criminal Court Dispositional Process: The Results of an Experiment," *The Journal of Criminal Law and Criminology* 75, no. 2 (1984): 493.

30. Ibid., 496–7.

31. Ibid.

32. Ibid., 498.

33. Ibid., 501.

34. Ibid., 500–1.

35. Ibid., 498.

36. Susan Howley and Carol Dorris, "Legal Rights for Crime Victims in the Criminal Justice System," in *Victims of Crime,* 3rd ed., ed. Robert C. Davis, Arthur J. Lurigio and Susan Herman (Thousand Oaks, CA: Sage Publications, 2007), 300.

37. Ibid.

38. Ibid., 300–1.

39. Ibid., 301.

40. Ibid.

41. Ibid., 300–3.

42. Ibid., 303.

43. Ibid., 300.

44. To identify states with strong legal rights, the authors analyzed state laws regarding the rights to restitution, to notification, to be present, and to be heard, as well as state constitutional protections for victims. A "strong" state ranked high on the basis of comprehensiveness, strength, and specificity. Dean G. Kilpatrick, David Beatty and Susan Smith Howley, *The Rights of Crime Victims—Does Legal Protection Make a Difference?* (Washington, DC: Department of Justice, National Institute of Justice, 1998), 3.

45. Ibid., 2–4.

46. Robert Elias, "Which Victim Movement? The Politics of Victim Policy," in *Victims of Crime: Problems, Policies, and Programs,* eds. Arthur J. Lurigio, Wesley G. Skogan and Robert C. Davis (Newbury Park, CA: Sage Publications, 1990), 242.

47. Kilpatrick, Beatty, and Howley, *The Rights of Crime Victims,* 4.

48. Howley and Dorris, "Legal Rights for Crime Victims in the Criminal Justice System," 311.

49. Ibid., 308–11

50. Ibid., 311.

51. For a more complete description of recent research about implementation of victims' rights refer to: Howley and Dorris, "Legal Rights for Crime Victims in the Criminal Justice System," 299–314.

52. Mark Scolforo, "States Step Up Demands for Restitution," FederalNewsRadio.com, Federal News Radio, www.federalnewsradio.com/?nid+80&pid=&sid=1315059&page=1.

53. Matt Krasnowski, "Crime Victims Due Money Falling Through The Cracks," *California Wire,* www.copleynews.com

54. Scolforo, "States Step Up Demands for Restitution."

55. Ibid.

56. Krasnowski, "Crime Victims Due Money Falling Through The Cracks."

57. Deborah P. Kelly and Edna Erez, "Victim Participation in the Criminal Justice System," in *Victims of Crime*, 2nd ed., eds. Robert C. Davis, Arthur J. Lurigio and Wesley G. Skogan (Thousand Oaks, CA: Sage Publications, 1997), 241.

58. Davis, Kunreuther, and Connick, "Expanding the Victim's Role in the Criminal Court Dispositional Process," 505.

59. Howard Zehr, *Changing Lenses: A New Focus for Crime and Justice* (Scottdale, PA: Herald Press, 1990), 178–214.

60. Howard Zehr, *The Little Book of Restorative Justice* (Intercourse, PA: Good Books, 2002), 37.

61. Ibid., 47–51.

62. An earlier version of this critique of restorative justice appeared in the following: Susan Herman, "Is Restorative Justice Possible Without a Parallel System for Victims?" in *Critical Issues In Restorative Justice,* eds. Howard Zehr and Barb Toews (Monsey, NY: Criminal Justice Press, 2004), 75–84.

63. See the following for a discussion of how the term " nonviolent" (as opposed to "financial"), defines a crime by what it isn't, and therefore diminishes its victims: Debbie Deem, Lisa Nerenberg, and Richard. Titus, "Victims of Financial Crime," in *Victims of Crime,* 2nd ed., eds. Robert C. Davis, Arthur J. Lurigio, and Susan Herman (Thousand Oaks, CA: Sage Publications, 2007), 138.

Chapter 3

1. In the rare circumstance when limited resources require restricting legal rights for victims, a more principled approach would be to distinguish between victims of felonies and victims of misdemeanors. For example, if it is absolutely necessary to restrict victims' rights, it would be more appropriate for a state to limit the right to confer with a prosecutor before a plea bargain to victims of felonies than to victims of violence.

CHAPTER 4

1. National Association of Crime Victim Compensation Boards, "Essential VOCA for Compensation Programs," Documents, www.nacvcb. org/articles/voca%20essential.final.htm.

2. Deborah Lamm Weisel, *Analyzing Repeat Victimization, Problem-Oriented Guides For Police-Problem Solving Tools Series No. 4* (Washington, DC: Department of Justice, Office of Community Oriented Policing Services, 2005), 7–11.

3. National Center for Victims of Crime and the Police Foundation, *Bringing Victims Into Community Policing* (Washington, DC: Department of Justice, Office of Community Oriented Policing Services, 2002), 14.

4. Weisel, *Analyzing Repeat Victimization,* 26–29.

5. David Forrester and others, *The Kirkholt Burglary Prevention Project, Rochdale,* Crime Prevention Unit Series Paper No. 13 (London, UK: Home Office Crime Prevention Unit, 1988), 16–17.

6. National Center for Victims of Crime and The Police Foundation, *Bringing Victims Into Community Policing,* 22.

7. Susan Howley and Carol Dorris, "Legal Rights for Crime Victims in the Criminal Justice System," in *Victims of Crime,* 3rd ed., ed. Robert C. Davis, Arthur J. Lurigio and Susan Herman (Thousand Oaks, CA: Sage Publications, 2007), 311.

8. Utah Code Title 41 Chapter 6a Section 1406(6)(c)(ii).

9. *Report on Survey of Crime Victims in Washington, DC* (Washington, DC: Metropolitan Police Department, 2002).

10. Joan Petersilia, *When Prisoners Come Home: Parole and Prisoner Reentry* (New York, NY: Oxford University Press, 2003), 163. By permission of Oxford University Press.

11. Susan Herman and Cressida Wasserman, "A Role for Victims in Offender Reentry" in *Crime and Delinquency* 47, No. 3 (2001): 431.

12. Howley and Dorris, "Legal Rights for Crime Victims in the Criminal Justice System," 301.

13. Anne K. Seymour, *The Victim's Role in Offender Reentry* (Washington, DC: Department of Justice, Office of Justice Programs, Office for Victims of Crime, 2001), 57–58.

14. See Seymour, *The Victim's Role in Offender Reentry,* 51-51, for guidelines for apologies.

15. Howard Zehr, "Saying I'm Sorry is Just the Beginning", *EMU News,* Eastern Mennonite University, www.emu.edu/nes/index.php/1349/cjp.

16. Howley and Dorris, "Legal Rights for Crime Victims in the Criminal Justice System", 306.

17. Caroline Wolf Harlow, *Prior Abuse Reported by Inmates and Probationers* (Washington, DC: Department of Justice, Office of Justice Programs, Bureau of Justice Statistics, 1999), 1–2.

18. New Hampshire General Court, "House Bill 0601," NH General Court Bill Status-2009 Chaptered Final Version, http://gencourt.state.nh.us/legislation/2009/HB0601.html (amended legislation effective as of September 14, 2009).

19. Pennsylvania Act 115: Domestic Violence Healthcare Response Act, 115, (1998).

20. University of Maryland Medical Center, "Study Shows That Hospital-Based Violence Intervention Program Can Reduce Rates of Injuries and Arrests," *Hospital-Based Violence Intervention Program,* www.umm.edu/news/releases/vip.htm.

21. See *Project Roadmap: Charting a Course for Crime Victims In Maryland* (Washington, DC: National Center for Victims of Crime, 2003) for an excellent analysis of how to improve the victim's rights laws in Maryland.

22. Deborah P. Kelly and Edna Erez, "Victim Participation in the Criminal Justice System," in *Victims of Crime,* 2nd ed., eds. Robert C. Davis, Arthur J. Lurigio and Wesley G. Skogan (Thousand Oaks, CA: Sage Publications, 1997), 241.

23. Illinois Compiled Statutes, Chapter 820, Section 180: Victims' Economic Security and Safety Act, 2003. (820 ILCS 180).

24. Official Code of Georgia Annotated, Title 34, Chapter 7, Subsection 7(b), 2007. [O.C.G. A. Section 34-1-7(b)].

25. Susan Herman and Michelle Waul, *Repairing the Harm: A New Vision for Crime Victim Compensation in America* (Washington, DC: National Center for Victims of Crime, 2004), 54.

26. Connecticut General Statutes Annotated: Title 54, Chapter 968 Section 54–210, 2000. (C.G.S.A. Section 54-210).

27. Susan Howley and Carol Dorris, "Legal Rights for Crime Victims in the Criminal Justice System," in *Victims of Crime*, 3rd ed., ed. Robert C. Davis, Arthur J. Lurigio and Susan Herman (Thousand Oaks, CA: Sage Publications, 2007), 309.

28. Ibid.

29. Ibid.

30. Restitution Report (Vermont: Vermont Center for Crime Victim Services, 2007), 1.

31. Herman and Waul, *Repairing the Harm*, 51.

32. Ibid., 52.

33. Violent Crime Control and Law Enforcement Act of 1994 (VCCLEA).

34. Department of Justice, Office of Justice Programs, Bureau of Justice Statistics, "Direct Expenditures by Level of Government, 1982–2006," *Key Facts At a Glance*, www.ojp.usdoj.gov/bjs/glance/tables/expgovtab.htm.

35. OVC Fact Sheet: *Victims of Crime Act Crime Victims Fund* (Washington, DC: Department of Justice, Office of Justice Programs, Office for Victims of Crime, 2005), 3.

36. There are some exceptions to this general rule that offenders' fines alone fund victim services and programs. Most notably, since 1994, Congress has appropriated between $300 and $500 million every year under the Violence Against Women Act. These funds have helped millions of women across America receive counseling, temporary housing, and critical support to escape violence. Garrine P. Laney, *The Violence Against Women Act: History and Federal Funding*, CRS Report for Congress (Washington, DC: Library of Congress, Congressional Research Service, 2005), 43–48.

CHAPTER 5

1. *Project Roadmap: Charting A Course for Crime Victims In Maryland* (Washington, DC: National Center for Victims of Crime, 2003).

Bibliography

"Anxiety Disorders: Traumatic Stress Disorders." In *DSM-IV-TR Mental Disorders: Diagnosis, Etiology,* edited by Michael B. First and Allan Tasman, 926–41. West Sussex, UK: John Wiley & Sons, Ltd., 2004.

Arata, Catalina M. "Child Sexual Abuse and Sexual Revictimization." *Clinical Psychology: Science and Practice* 9, no. 2 (2002): 135–64.

Baum, Katrina. *Identity Theft, 2005.* Washington, DC: Department of Justice, Office of Justice Programs, Bureau of Justice Statistics, 2007.

Black Homicide Victimization in the United States: An Analysis of 2006 Homicide Data. Washington, DC: Violence Policy Center, 2009.

Bybee, Deborah and Cris M. Sullivan. "Predicting Re-Victimization of Battered Women 3 Years After Exiting a Shelter Program." *American Journal of Community Psychology* 36, nos. 1, 2 (2005): 85–96.

Centers for Disease Control and Prevention, National Center for Injury Prevention and Control, Office of Statistics and Programming. "10 Leading Causes of Death, United States, 2006, Black, Both Sexes." http://webappa.cdc.gov/sasweb/ncipc/leadcaus10.html.

Conley, Carey Thomson, Kevin Roberts, Andrew Curran, Louise Ryan, and Rosalind J. Wright. "Caretaker-Child Concordance for Child's Exposure to Violence in a Preadolescent Inner-City Population." *Archives of Pediatrics & Adolescent Medicine* 156, no. 8 (2008): 818–23.

Connecticut General Statutes Annotated: Title 54, Chapter 968 Section 54-210, 2000. (C.G.S.A. Section 54-210).

Costs of Intimate Partner Violence Against Women in the United States. Atlanta, GA: Department of Health and Human Services, Centers For Disease Control and Prevention, National Center for Injury Prevention and Control, 2003.

Council of State Governments Eastern Regional Conference. *What Do We Want (and What Are We Getting) From the Criminal Justice System?* New York: Council of State Governments, 1999.

Criminal Victimization in the United States, 1973. Washington, DC: Department of Justice, Law Enforcement Assistance Administration, National Criminal Justice Information and Statistics Service, 1976.

Criminal Victimization in the United States, 2005 Statistical Tables. Washington, DC: Department of Justice, Office of Justice Programs, Bureau of Justice Statistics, 2006.

Daigle, Leah E., Bonnie S. Fisher, and Pamela Guthrie. "The Reoccurrence of Victimization." In *Victims of Crime,* 3rd ed., edited by Robert C. Davis, Arthur J. Lurigio and Susan Herman, 211–32. Thousand Oaks, CA: Sage Publications, 2007.

Davis, Robert C., Frances Kunreuther and Elizabeth Connick. "Expanding the Victim's Role in the Criminal Court Dispositional Process: The Results of an Experiment." *The Journal of Criminal Law and Criminology* 75, no. 2 (1984): 491–505.

Davis, Robert C. *Impact Evaluation of the Victim/Witness Assistance Project's Appearance Management Activities.* New York: Vera Institute of Justice, 1976.

——— "Mediation: The Brooklyn Experiment." In *Neighborhood Justice: Assessment of an Emerging Idea,* edited by R. Tomasic and M.M. Feeley, 154-71. New York: Longman, 1982.

——— "Victim/Witness Noncooperation: A Second Look At A Persistent Phenomenon." *Journal of Criminal Justice* 11, no. 4 (1983): 287–99.

Deem, Debbie, Lisa Nerenberg, and Richard Titus. "Victims of Financial Crime." In *Victims of Crime,* 3rd ed., edited by Robert C. Davis, Arthur J. Lurigio and Susan Herman, 125–45. Thousand Oaks, CA: Sage Publications, 2007.

Dugan, Laura. "The Effect of Criminal Victimization on a Household's Moving Decision." *Criminology* 37, no. 4 (1999): 903–30.

Elias, Robert. "Which Victim Movement? The Politics of Victim Policy." In *Victims of Crime: Problems, Policies, and Programs,* edited by Arthur J. Lurigio, Wesley G. Skogan and Robert C. Davis, 226-50. Newbury Park, CA: Sage Publications, 1990.

Ellingworth, Dan, Graham Farrell, and Ken Pease. "A Victim Is A Victim Is A Victim? Chronic Victimization in Four Sweeps of the British Crime Survey." *British Journal of Criminology* 35, no. 3 (1995): 360–5.

Farrell, Graham and Adam C. Bouloukos. "International Overview: A Cross-National Comparison of Rates of Repeat Victimization." In *Repeat Victimization.* Crime Prevention Studies, Volume 12, edited by Graham Farrell and Ken Pease, 2–25. Monsey, NY: Criminal Justice Press, 2001.

Farrell, Graham and Ken Pease. *Once Bitten, Twice Bitten: Repeat Victimization and its Implications for Crime Prevention.* Crime Prevention Unit Series Paper No. 46. London, UK: Home Office Police Research Group, 1993.

Finkelhor, David and Jennifer Dziuba-Leatherman. "Children as Victims of Violence: A National Survey." *Pediatrics* 94, no. 4 (1994): 413–20.

Finkelhor, David, Richard Ormrod, Heather Turner, and Sherry A. Hamby. "Victimization of Children and Youth: A Comprehensive, National Survey." *Child Maltreatment* 10, no. 1 (2005): 5–25.

Fitzpatrick, Kevin M. and Janet P. Boldizar. "The Prevalence and Consequences of Exposure to Violence Among African-American Youth." *Journal of the American Academy of Child and Adolescent Psychiatry* 32 (1993): 424–30.

Forrester, David, Mike Chatterton, and Ken Pease. *The Kirkholt Burglary Prevention Project, Rochdale.* Crime Prevention Unit Series Paper No. 13. London, UK: Home Office Crime Prevention Unit, 1988.

"The Fundamentals of Mental Health and Mental Illness." In *Mental Health: A Report of the Surgeon General.* Rockville, MD: Department of Health and Human Services, U.S. Public Health Service, 1999, table 2.6.

Ganzini, Linda, Benston McFarland, and Joseph Bloom. "Victims of Fraud: Comparing Victims of White Collar and Violent Crime." *Bulletin of the American Academy of Psychiatry and the Law* 18, no. 1 (1990): 55–63.

Gondolf, Edward E. "The Effect of Batterer Counseling On Shelter Outcome." *Journal of Interpersonal Violence* 3, no. 3 (1988): 275–89.

Hanmer, Jalna and Elizabeth Stanko. "Stripping Away the Rhetoric of Protection: Violence to Women, Law and the State in Britain and the USA." *International Journal of the Sociology of Law* 13 (1985): 357–74.

Hanson, Rochelle F., Dean G. Kilpatrick, Sherry A. Falsetti, and Heide S. Resnick. "Violent Crime and Mental Health." In *Traumatic Stress: From Theory To Practice. Plenum Series On Stress and Coping,* edited by John R. Freedy and Stevan E. Hobfoll, 129–62. New York: Springer, 1995.

Hart, Timothy C. and Callie Rennison. *Reporting Crime to the Police, 1992–2000.* Washington, DC: Department of Justice, Office of Justice Programs, Bureau of Justice Statistics, 2003.

Herman, Judith Lewis. *Trauma and Recovery.* New York: Basic Books, 1992.

Herman, Susan. "Is Restorative Justice Possible Without a Parallel System for Victims?" In *Critical Issues In Restorative Justice,* edited by Howard Zehr and Barb Toews, 75–84. Monsey, NY: Criminal Justice Press, 2004.

Herman, Susan and Michelle Waul. *Repairing the Harm: A New Vision for Crime Victim Compensation in America.* Washington, DC: National Center for Victims of Crime, 2004.

Howley, Susan and Carol Dorris. "Legal Rights for Crime Victims in the Criminal Justice System." In *Victims of Crime,* 3rd ed., edited by Robert C. Davis, Arthur J. Lurigio and Susan Herman, 299–314. Thousand Oaks, CA: Sage Publications, 2007.

Illinois Compiled Statutes, Chapter 820, Section 180: Victims' Economic Security and Safety Act, 2003. (820 ILCS 180).

Kennedy, David. *Deterrence and Crime Prevention.* New York: Routledge, 2009.

Klaus, Patsy. *Crimes Against Persons Age 65 or Older, 1993–2002.* Washington, DC: Department of Justice, Office of Justice Programs, Bureau of Justice Statistics, 2005.

Kleemans, Edward R. "Repeat Burglary Victimization: Results of Empirical Research in the Netherlands." In *Repeat Victimization. Crime Prevention Studies* Volume 12, edited by Graham Farrell and Ken Pease, 53–68. Monsey, NY: Criminal Justice Press, 2001.

Kilpatrick, Dean G. and Ron Acierno. "Mental Health Needs of Crime Victims: Epidemiology and Outcomes." *Journal of Traumatic Stress* 16, no. 2 (2003): 119–32.

Kilpatrick, Dean G. *The Mental Health Impact of Rape.* National Violence Against Women Prevention Research Center. www.musc.edu/vawprevention/research/mentalimpact.

Karmen, Andrew. *Crime Victim: An Introduction to Victimology.* 4th ed. Belmont, CA: Wadsworth Thomson Learning, 2001.

Kelly, Deborah P. and Edna Erez. "Victim Participation in the Criminal Justice System." In *Victims of Crime,* 2nd ed., edited by Robert C. Davis, Arthur J. Lurigio and Wesley G. Skogan, 231–56. Thousand Oaks, CA: Sage Publications, 1997.

Kilpatrick, Dean G., David Beatty and Susan Howley. *The Rights of Crime Victims—Does Legal Protection Make a Difference?* Washington, DC: Department of Justice, National Institute of Justice, 1998.

Krasnowski, Matt. "Crime Victims Due Money Falling Through Cracks." *California Wire.* www.copleynews.com.

Labriola, Melissa, Michael Rampel and Robert C. Davis. *Testing the Effectiveness of Batterer Programs and Judicial Monitoring.* New York: Center for Court Innovation, 2005.

Laney, Garrine P. *Violence Against Women Act: History and Federal Funding.* CRS Report for Congress. Washington, DC: Library of Congress, Congressional Research Service, 2005.

Lloyd, Sam, Graham Farrell and Ken Pease. *Preventing Repeated Domestic Violence: A Demonstration Project on Merseyside.* Crime Prevention Unit Series Paper No. 49. London, UK: Home Office Police Department, 1994.

McKinnon, Jesse. *The Black Population in the United States: March 2002.* Washington, DC: Department of Commerce, Economics and Statistics Administration, U.S. Census Bureau, 2003.

Miller, Ted R., Mark A. Cohen, and Brian Wiersema. *Victim Costs and Consequences: A New Look.* Washington, DC: Department of Justice, National Institute of Justice, 1996.

Morgan, Frank. "Repeat Burglary in a Perth Suburb." In *Repeat Victimization. Crime Prevention Studies* Volume 12, edited by Graham Farrell and Ken Pease, 83–118. Monsey, NY: Criminal Justice Press, 2001.

National Association of Crime Victim Compensation Boards. "Essential VOCA for Compensation Programs." Documents. www.nacvcb.org/articles/voca%20essential.final.htm.

National Center for Victims of Crime and the Police Foundation. *Bringing Victims Into Community Policing.* Washington, DC: Department of Justice, Office of Community Oriented Policing Services, 2002.

Project Roadmap: Charting A Course for Crime Victims In Maryland. Washington, DC: National Center for Victims of Crime, 2003.

New Directions for the Field: Victims' Rights and Services for the 21st Century. Washington, DC: Department of Justice, Office of Justice Programs, Office for Victims of Crime, 1998.

New Hampshire General Court. "House Bill 0601." NH General Court Bill Status-2009 Chaptered Final Version. http://gencourt.state.nh.us/legislation/2009/HB0601.html.

Newmark, Lisa, Judy Bonderman, Barbara Smith, and E. Blaine Liner. *The National Evaluation of State Victims of Crime Act Assistance and Compensation Programs: Trends and Strategies for the Future.* Washington, DC: Urban Institute, 2003.

Official Code of Georgia Annotated, Title 34, Chapter 7, Subsection 7(b), 2007. (O.C.G.A. 34-1-7(b).

OVC Fact Sheet: *Victims of Crime Act Crime Victims Fund.* Washington, DC: Department of Justice, Office of Justice Programs, Office for Victims of Crime 2005.

Pennsylvania Act 115: Domestic Violence Healthcare Response Act, 115 (1998).

Perry, Steven W. *American Indians and Crime.* Washington, DC: Department of Justice, Office of Justice Programs, Bureau of Justice Statistics, 2004.

Petersilia, Joan. *When Prisoners Come Home: Parole and Prisoner Reentry.* New York, NY: Oxford University Press, 2003.

Rand, Michael. *Criminal Victimization, 2007.* Washington, DC: Department of Justice, Office of Justice Programs, Bureau of Justice Statistics, 2008.

Report on Survey of Crime Victims in Washington, DC Washington, DC: Metropolitan Police Department, 2002.

Restitution Report. Vermont: Vermont Center for Crime Victim Services, 2007.

Ruback, R. Barry and Martie P. Thompson. *Social and Psychological Consequences of Violent Victimization.* Thousand Oaks, CA: Sage Publications, 2001.

Sampson, Robert J. "The Community," in *Crime: Public Policies For Crime Control,* edited by James Q. Wilson and Joan Petersilia, 225–52. Oakland, CA: Institute for Contemporary Studies, 2002.

Scolforo, Mark. "States Step Up Demands for Restitution." FederalNewsRadio. com. *Federal News Radio.* www.federalnewsradio.com/?nid+80&pid= &sid=1315059&page=1.

Seymour, Anne K. *The Victim's Role in Offender Reentry.* Washington, DC: Department of Justice, Office of Justice Programs, Office for Victims of Crime, 2001.

Shaffer, Jennifer N. and R. Barry Ruback. *Violent Victimization as a Risk Factor for Violent Offending Among Juveniles.* Washington, DC: Department of Justice, Office of Justice Programs, Office of Juvenile Delinquency, 2002.

Silverman, Jay G., Anita Raj, Lorelei A. Mucci, and Jeanne E. Hathaway. "Dating Violence Against Adolescent Girls and Associated Substance Use, Unhealthy Weight Control, Sexual Risk Behavior, Pregnancy, and Suicidality." *Journal of the American Medical Association* 286, no. 5 (2001): 572–79.

Stark, Evan and Anne Flitcraft. *Women at Risk: Domestic Violence and Women's Health.* Thousand Oaks, CA: Sage Publications, 1996.

Synovate. *Federal Trade Commission-Identity Theft Report.* Washington, DC: Federal Trade Commission, 2003.

Synovate. *Federal Trade Commission-2006 Identity Theft Report.* Washington, DC: Federal Trade Commission, 2007.

Taylor, L., B. Zuckerman, V. Harik, and B. M. Groves. "Witnessing Violence By Young Children and Their Mothers." *Journal of Developmental and Behavioral Pediatrics* 15, no. 2 (1994): 120–123.

Travis, Jeremy. *But They All Come Back: Facing the Challenges of Prisoner Reentry.* Washington, DC: The Urban Institute Press, 2005.

University of Maryland Medical Center. "Study Shows That Hospital-Based Violence Intervention Program Can Reduce Rates of Injuries and Arrests." *Hospital-Based Violence Intervention Program.* www.umm. edu/news/releases/vip.htm.

U.S. Code-Title 42 Section 10602: Crime Victim Compensation.

Department of Justice, Federal Bureau of Investigation, Criminal Justice Information Services Division. "Crime in the United States by Volume and Rate Per 100,000 Inhabitants 1988-2007." *Crime in the United States 2007.* www.fbi.gov/ucr/cius2007/data/table_01.html.

Department of Justice-Federal Bureau of Investigation. "Expanded Homicide Data Table 2- Murder Victims by Age, Sex, and Race 2007." *Crime in the United States 2007.* www.fbi.gov/ucr/cius07/offenses/expanded_information/data/shrtable_02.html.

Department of Justice, Office of Justice Programs, Bureau of Justice Statistics. "Direct Expenditures by Level of Government, 1982–2006." *Key Facts at a Glance.* www.ojp.usdoj.gov/bjs/glance/tables/expgovtab.htm.

Department of Justice, Office of Justice Programs, National Institute of Justice. "Victim Satisfaction With The Criminal Justice System." *National Institute of Justice Journal,* no. 253 (2006).www.ojp.usdoj.gov/nij/journals/253/victim.html.

Department of Justice, Office of Justice Programs, Office for Victims of Crime. "1998 Victims of Crime Act of 1884 Performance Report State Compensation Program." *Nationwide Analysis-Victims of Crime Act.* www.ojp.usdoj.gov/ovc/fund/vocanpr_vc98_1.html.

Department of Justice, Office of Justice Programs, Office for Victims of Crime. "2006 Victims of Crime Act of 1984 Performance Report State Compensation Program." *Nationwide Analysis-Victims of Crime Act.* www.ojp.usdoj.gov/ovc/fund/vocanpr_vc06.html.

Utah Code Title 41 Chapter 6a Section 1406(6)(c)(ii).

"Victims of Crime Act Victim Compensation Grant Program." *Federal Registrar* 66, no. 95 (2001): 27158–166.

Violent Crime Control and Law Enforcement Act of 1994 (VCCLEA).

Weisel, Deborah Lamm. *Analyzing Repeat Victimization. Problem-Oriented Guides For Police-Problem Solving Tools* Series No. 4. Washington, DC: Department of Justice, Office of Community Oriented Policing Services, 2005.

Widom, Cathy Spatz, and Michael G. Maxfield. *An Update On the "Cycle of Violence."* Washington, DC: Department of Justice, Office of Justice Programs, National Institute of Justice, 2001.

Widom, Cathy Spatz. "The Cycle of Violence." *Science* 244, no. 4901 (1989): 162.

Wilson, James Q. "Crime and Public Policy." In *Crime: Public Policies For Crime Control,* edited by James Q. Wilson and Joan Petersilia, 537–57. Oakland, CA: Institute for Contemporary Studies, 2002.

Wolf Harlow, Caroline. *Prior Abuse Reported by Inmates and Probationers.* Washington, DC: Department of Justice, Office of Justice Programs, Bureau of Justice Statistics, 1999.

Wordes, Madeline and Michelle Nunez. *Our Vulnerable Teenagers: Their Victimization, Its Consequences, and Directions for Prevention and Intervention.* Washington, DC: National Center for Victims of Crime, 2002.

Young, Marlene A. *Meeting Victim Needs: What Is The Role Of Victim Compensation In Recovery?* Washington, DC: National Center for Victims of Crime, 2003.

Zehr, Howard. *Changing Lenses: A New Focus for Crime and Justice.* Scottdale, PA: Herald Press, 1990.

——— "Saying I'm Sorry is Just the Beginning." *EMU News.* Eastern Mennonite University. www.emu.edu/nes/index.php/1349/cjp.

——— *The Little Book of Restorative Justice.* Intercourse, PA: Good Books, 2002.

Acknowledgments

Special thanks to my colleagues at the National Center for Victims of Crime, particularly Mary Rappaport, Michael Kaiser, Jim Ferguson, Susan Howley, and Michelle Waul Webster who encouraged me to develop the principles of Parallel Justice, to Mary Lou Leary who later continued the center's commitment to Parallel Justice, and David Austern who was always there when I needed him.

While I developed the concept of Parallel Justice at the National Center for Victims of Crime, I wrote this book while teaching at Pace University. I thank Pace for creating an environment that allowed me to pursue this project.

Three people provided critical research support: Michelle Waul Webster conducted important early research and helped create the structure of the book; Natalia Gouz generously served as my research assistant throughout most of the writing of the book; and Aliza Travis joined the team in the homestretch to update some of the initial research. Thank you.

Several people read early drafts of the manuscript and provided invaluable comments. For their careful reading and thoughtful critiques I thank Mary Achilles, Sharon Davis, Ida Dupont, Jerilyn Fisher, Martin Horn, Doug Katz, Christian Pfeiffer, Mary Rappaport, Judy Rex, Cressida Wasserman, Michelle Waul Webster, Barbara Whitchurch, and Howard Zehr. And a very special thanks to Pat James who just couldn't read it without editing it. Thank goodness!

For all the right advice exactly when I needed it, I thank Judith Appelbaum.

I am also grateful for Cynthia Frank's guidance and Michael Brechner's clean book design.

Special thanks go to Doug Katz, for his persistent encouragement and his beautiful cover art.

Several colleagues have been particularly important along the way. Thanks to everyone working on Parallel Justice in Burlington, particularly Judy Rex, Sharon Davis, Karen Vastine, Barbara Whitchurch, and Cara Gleason for allowing me to journey alongside you. Thank you Jim Bueermann for incorporating Parallel Justice into your vision of policing, Frank Ochberg for our many conversations about trauma, Howard Zehr for urging me to "turn it into a book," David Kennedy for helping me appreciate the power of paradigms, and Lucy Friedman for your pioneering work with victims of crime.

Special thanks to Joann Lang whose generous contribution helped publish this book.

My children, Aliza and Zoe Travis, understood and celebrated my commitment to this project. I will always be grateful for their enthusiastic support.

Finally, my most profound thanks are for my husband, Jeremy Travis, without whom I would never have started or finished this book.

⊣ | | | ⊢

Index

About the Author

Susan Herman is an associate professor in the Department of Criminal Justice at Pace University. From 1997 to 2004, Ms. Herman served as the executive director of the National Center for Victims of Crime, the nation's leading resource and advocacy organization for crime victims. While at the National Center for Victims of Crime, Ms. Herman developed a new framework for society's response to victims called Parallel Justice and first introduced the concept in a speech at the National Press Club. With more than 25 years of leadership experience in government, criminal justice, and social services, Ms. Herman is an internationally recognized spokesperson for victims of crime and Parallel Justice.

Previously, Ms. Herman served as Director of Community Services at The Enterprise Foundation, Director of the Domestic Violence Division of Victim Services (now Safe Horizon) in New York City, Special Counsel to the Police Commissioner of New York City, Director of Mediation Services at the Institute for Mediation and Conflict Resolution, as an attorney at the NOW Legal Defense and Education Fund, and as an instructor at New York University's School of Law and NYU's Wagner School of Public Service. Ms. Herman is a graduate of Bryn Mawr College and the Antioch School of Law.